The Seattle Bride
Wedding Planner

✴

published by Tiger Oak Publications

Text by Linda Henry

Layout by Courtney Colwell

✳

Created and produced by Tiger Oak Publications

Editor: Susan Bonne

Design/Art Direction: Alicia Nammacher

Associate Editor: Beth Rutledge

Associate Art Director: Cathy Nemecek

Editorial Assistant: Amie Duhamel

Administration: Dilek Aydinalp

Copyright 1998
Tiger Oak Publications, Inc.
123 North Third Street, Suite 508
Minneapolis, Minnesota 55401

All rights reserved. No part of this publication may be reproduced, stored in a retrieval system or transmitted in any form or by any means, electronic, mechanical, photocopying, recording, or otherwise, without the prior written permission of Tiger Oak Publications.

First printing: July 1998
Printed in U.S.A.

ISBN 0-9663558-0-6

Preface

✶ ✶ ✶ ✶ ✶

Although your wedding ceremony and reception occupy just a few fleeting hours, arranging the festivities will be remembered as an era of your life. It's a period of weeks or months in which you'll learn much about what's important to yourself, to your partner, and to the two of you as a couple. The *Seattle Bride Wedding Planner* is a practical workbook that's intended for both the bride and the groom. Each section covers one aspect of the wedding, from setting a budget and compiling the guest list, to setting the date and writing your vows, through dressing the wedding party and packing for your honeymoon. Along the way, recent newlyweds offer creative ideas and been-there advice. After the ceremony, this wedding planner will serve as a keepsake—a scrapbook of your first creative joint venture as bride and groom. In the whirlwind of preparations, don't forget to enjoy yourselves. Planning a wedding can be stressful at times, but overall it should be a joyful experience. In fact, this is advice that will serve you well in marriage: Remember to have fun.

Seattle Bride Magazine

✶ ✶ ✶ ✶ ✶

Table of Contents

* * * * *

PLANNER AT A GLANCE 4
   An abbreviated checklist of wedding-related tasks

GETTING STARTED

A BUDGET YOU CAN LIVE WITH 9
   What's the Bottom Line? / What? The Sky's Not the Limit? / Need Some Help? / Cost-Cutting Wedding Tips / Wedding Expenses Worksheet

INVITATIONS, PROGRAMS & ANNOUNCEMENTS 14
   Negotiating the Number / No Regrets / Compiling the Master Guest List / Composing Your Invites / Printers' Estimates / The Guest List / Thank-You Notes / Wedding Programs / Announcements List

THE CEREMONY

THE CEREMONY 31
   Who Will Be Officiating? / Where Will We Be Married? / Setting the Date / Choosing Your Wedding Party / The Vows / Site Planning and Decor / Don't Forget to Bring… / Ceremony Timetable

THE RECEPTION

THE RECEPTION 37
   Selecting a Site / Elements of Style / Catering / The Wedding Cake / Reception Decor / Reception Timetable

WEDDING ATTIRE

WEDDING ATTIRE 49
   Bride's Attire / Something Old / Bride's Attendants / Flower Girl / The Mothers / Groom's Attire / Groom's Attendants / Ringbearer

THE RINGS 60
   The Engagement Ring / The Four Cs / Precious Metals / His Wedding Ring, Her Wedding Ring / Choosing a Reputable Jeweler

* * * * *

Table of Contents

* * * * *

Services

Transportation **65**
   For Out-of-Town Guests / Parking / Making a Grand Entrance / Choosing a Transportation Company

Flowers **70**
   Finding a Florist / Flowers for the Wedding Party / Flowers for the Ceremony / Flowers for the Reception / The Floral Plan

Music **76**
   The Ceremony / Music Sources / The Reception

Photography & Videography **82**
   Choosing a Photographer / Narrowing the Field / Choosing a Videographer

Gifts, Parties & Honeymoon

Giving & Receiving Gifts **89**
   Chart for Recording Gifts / Gift Registry / Thank-Yous / List of Thank-Yous

Parties **102**
   The Engagement Party / The Bridesmaids' Party / The Rehearsal Dinner / The Gift-Opening Brunch

Your Honeymoon **107**
   Bon Voyage / Wedding Night Bliss / Honeymoon Possibilities / Travel Information & Itinerary / What to Pack

Resources

Resources **113**
   Your guide to the region's best local providers.

* * * * *

Planner At A Glance

The key to a flawless wedding lies in the preparation. A well-orchestrated plan can act as a map of the big event; knowing what you've already accomplished and what comes next can help to ease your mind and get you ready. It's your job to chart the course that will turn a lifetime's worth of thoughts and ideas into blissful wedding-day reality. (No pressure there.) Of course, you can't be responsible for everything; learn to delegate as necessary. Let the following checklist serve as a guide to keep you on the straight and narrow and get you down the aisle.

9 to 12 Months	☐ Announce your engagement. ☐ Set the date/choose a location. (Be prepared for a possible compromise. If the date is critically important, you may have to settle for a second-choice location. If location is more meaningful, keep an open mind about the date.) ☐ Create a wedding budget. ☐ Choose your attendants. ☐ Begin shopping for your gown and the bridesmaids' dresses. ☐ Hire a wedding coordinator, if you so desire.
6 to 9 Months	☐ Decide on the number of guests. Start compiling a list, and ask both the groom's mother and your mother to do the same. ☐ Book the photographer, band/D.J., caterers, florist and videographer. ☐ Begin a list of favorite music and requested songs to give to the band or D.J. ☐ Choose an officiant. ☐ Go with the groom to a formalwear store or tailor. After the groom's attire has been chosen, the groom should encourage the ushers and groomsmen to go in and get fitted as soon as possible.
4 to 6 Months	☐ Order invitations, napkins, programs, etc. ☐ Choose your wedding bands. (A growing trend: "Surprising" the groom with your choice for his ring or choosing his ring from several that you know he likes. Isn't this what he did when you got engaged?) ☐ Ask your mother to shop for her dress. After she's bought hers, the groom's mother can choose her attire. ☐ Talk with your parents—and his—to find out if you should reserve hotel rooms for out-of-town guests.

4 to 6 Months (cont.)	☐ Arrange a time for the wedding rehearsal. ☐ Start planning the rehearsal dinner with your intended. ☐ Meet with a travel agent to plan the honeymoon. ☐ Book wedding-night accommodations and transportation for you and your groom.
2 to 4 Months	☐ Have alterations completed on your gown. Try on all of the accessories to be sure that everything "works." ☐ Book a final fitting, start breaking in your shoes. ☐ Finish alterations on bridesmaids' dresses. ☐ Consult with florist, photographer, D.J., etc. to confirm contracts and be sure that everything is in order. ☐ Make appointments for hair, manicure, make-up. (Include at least one pre-wedding-day appointment to "rehearse" make-up and hairstyle.) ☐ Shop for bridesmaids' gifts. Ask the groom to shop for groomsmen's gifts. ☐ Register for wedding gifts. ☐ Begin addressing invitations. Take one to the post office and have it weighed to ensure proper postage. ☐ Set aside one day for personal pampering. Take a day off from work, get a massage, go to a coffeehouse. Relax—it may be the last time for a while that you can do so.
6 to 8 Weeks	☐ Mail the invitations. ☐ Finalize rehearsal dinner details. ☐ Call hotels to confirm reservations for out-of-town guests and your wedding night. ☐ Confirm honeymoon travel plans. ☐ Start delegating smaller tasks to your Maid of Honor, attendants. Can someone pick up candles, clear nail polish, ribbon, balloons? ☐ Pick up the rings and check the engraving. ☐ Arrange to have your gown pressed and tell the shop when you'll be picking it up. ☐ Get your marriage license.

Planner at a Glance

3 to 6 Weeks	☐	Plan seating arrangements for the reception.
	☐	Think about packing for the honeymoon. Remind the groom.
	☐	Speak with the D.J./band about important musical requests. Confirm that everything is to your satisfaction.
	☐	Speak with the coordinator at the reception site to find out what time the cake and flowers can be delivered on the wedding day. Ask if deliveries should be made at a special entrance.
	☐	Talk with the photographer to confirm what time you need to be prepared for pictures on the big day.
	☐	Check over all of your contracts. When are payments due? Have all contract requirements been met?
	☐	If at all possible, indulge in a weekend getaway with your fella. Stay in a B&B. Watch the leaves change/snow fall/sun shine. Frolic. Remember why you want to spend the rest of your life with this man. Don't fret about the wedding.
2 Weeks	☐	If you'd like your wedding announced in the newspaper, call the paper for information.
	☐	Arrange for your fiancé to be made beneficiary of your life insurance. If you each have health insurance through your employers, choose the plan that's best suited for both of you and make arrangements accordingly.
	☐	If you're changing your name, contact the DMV, your bank, credit cards and Social Security.
	☐	If possible, begin writing checks for the officiant, photographer, videographer, etc. No one involved with the wedding will want to be filling out checks on the big day.
	☐	Put someone in charge of all the gifts brought to the reception. This person (or persons) will be responsible for transporting them at the end of the evening.
1 Week	☐	Notify the caterer of the final guest count.
	☐	Go over last-minute details with florist, musicians, etc.
	☐	Take a few minutes to write a note to his parents and yours, thanking them for their love and support. Put stamps on the envelopes. Drop them in the mail.

Planner at a Glance

1 Week (cont.)	☐ Put together everything you'll need for the wedding day: Something old, something new, something borrowed, something blue. Include your jewelry, an extra pair of pantyhose, aspirin, antacid, bobby pins, safety pins, mints, your undergarments. This is your personal crisis kit. Don't leave for the ceremony without it.
3 Days	☐ Speak to the head usher about unique seating arrangements or guests with special needs. ☐ Give the marriage license to the Maid of Honor or Best Man and remind this person to bring it to the ceremony. ☐ If you'll be paying your officiant at the wedding, put the check in a sealed envelope and give it to the Best Man. Remind him to bring the envelope with him on the big day. ☐ Tell the attendants and parents what time they'll need to arrive at the rehearsal. Give your bridesmaids their gifts at the rehearsal dinner. ☐ All of the details are done. Forget about the logistics of the impending event and try to enjoy what's going on around you. ☐ Begin greeting your out-of-town guests. ☐ Remember to eat. ☐ Try to get some rest.
The Wedding Day	☐ Eat something for breakfast. ☐ If you haven't already, give your Maid of Honor the groom's wedding band. ☐ See your stylist for final preparations. ☐ Gather all of your pre-packed belongings and head for the altar. ☐ Get there on time. ☐ Relax. Enjoy. Congratulations—you made it.

Planner at a Glance

Notes

* * * *

Getting Started

GETTING STARTED

A BUDGET YOU
CAN LIVE WITH

✹

INVITATIONS, PROGRAMS
& ANNOUNCEMENTS

A Budget You Can Live With

✶ ✶ ✶ ✶ ✶

Getting Started

A bride and groom today can celebrate the beginning of their marriage in a thousand different ways, with promises exchanged in a simple country chapel or with proclamations made before 500 of their closest friends and business associates. In either case, the vows are equally heartfelt. So don't be discouraged by estimates like those offered by *Modern Bride* magazine, which state that the average cost of an American wedding with 200 guests now approaches $20,000. The fact is that every year thousands of couples celebrate their nuptials for less than that, while a few others add a sixth digit to that figure. Only you can determine the amount of money you want to spend on your wedding.

What's the Bottom Line?

The obvious sources for financing the wedding are the bride's family, the groom's family, the couple themselves, or some combination thereof; traditionally, the bride's family paid for the wedding, while the groom's family hosted the groom's dinner. But more and more couples are taking on at least some, if not all, of the financial responsibility. The greatest benefit of paying for the event yourselves is that there's no question about doing things your way. On the other hand, no one should go deeply into debt paying for a wedding—least of all a young couple just starting out.

As a couple, look at your finances and determine what you can afford to spend. The next part gets tricky. Approach parents—if they are willing and able to help—and ask them whether, and how much, they'd be willing to contribute. This may be uncomfortable; you're dealing with the relative wealth of two sets of relatives. (If the groom's family follows tradition, they will likely offer to host the rehearsal dinner.) The important thing is to obtain a specific dollar amount that each resource is willing to put forth. Add up all the contributions, and you have your wedding budget.

What? The Sky's Not the Limit?

Look at it this way—if you could spend as much money as you wanted, you would be deprived the opportunity to examine your priorities. So what are they? Is it great food for a few of your closest friends and relatives, a top-notch photographer, a designer dress? How much will that cost? What's left over? Does that change your priorities?

Your budget will influence the number of guests you invite and the style of your wedding. The easiest way to keep costs down is to limit the number of guests. Whatever your budget, hold fast to your vision of what your wedding day will be like—whether you want the reception to include a formal sit-down dinner or a casual barbecue on the beach. Expenses can be cut painlessly in a variety of ways.

✴ ✴ ✴ ✴ ✴

Morning and afternoon receptions are less expensive than evening affairs. Friends or family members may be willing to contribute certain elements, be it a backyard reception site or an heirloom dress. Those with special talents may be willing to volunteer services as seamstress, photographer, videographer, cake-baker or caterer.

Need Some Help?

At this point you may feel overwhelmed by the prospect of planning the entire wedding yourself. Take heart—that's why bridal shows and wedding consultants were invented.

In addition to fashion shows and exhibits, bridal shows often offer vendor discounts and prizes—everything from vacuum cleaners to $2,000 gowns. Check with local bridal associations or area department stores and malls, who also host occasional events.

Wedding consultants can provide assistance in small or large doses, and you shouldn't assume that the cost is out of reach. Since consultants know where to find the good deals, they might even save you money. A two-hour consultation typically runs from $100 to $300; full-service consulting can cost $1,000 to $2,500, or 10 to 15 percent for very extravagant weddings.

Use the worksheet on page 11 to assemble a comprehensive list of your expenses.

There will be some items that won't apply to you and your wedding (that's money saved), and you might want to add others that are not included here (space is provided for additional expenses at the end of the list). For the purpose of apportioning your budget, fill out the first column, "Preliminary Estimate." As a general guideline, you can apportion 40 to 50 percent to the reception, 10 percent to bridalwear, and 20 percent to the honeymoon. At this point you should also be able to fill out the second column, "To Be Paid By." As you talk to vendors and put in place the various elements, you can return to this chart and record estimates, deposits and balances paid. Be sure to save your receipts.

Remember, your budget should determine your expenses, not the other way around.

Cost-Cutting Wedding Tips

✳ *Limit the guest list.*

✳ *Schedule the wedding during "off-peak" times. You'll pay top dollar for a Saturday-night wedding in September, now one of the most popular months to be wed. Fridays and Sundays are less popular and thus less expensive. The off-peak wedding season runs November to April.*

✳ *Enlist friends and family members to volunteer their services.*

✳ *An open bar creates an unpredictable expense. Instead, offer wine and champagne.*

Wedding Expenses Worksheet

	Preliminary Estimate	To Be Paid By	Vendor's Estimate	Deposit Amt.	Date Paid	Balance Due	Date Paid
Bridal Consultant							
Wedding Attire							
Bride's Dress							
Headpiece							
Shoes							
Hair Stylist							
Make-up							
Manicure							
Groom's Tux/Suit							
Shoes							
Hair Stylist							
Manicure							
Bride's Attendants							
Groom's Attendants							
Printing							
Invitations							
postage							
Reply Cards							
postage							
Programs							
Announcements							
postage							
Thank-you Notes							
postage							
Napkins							
Matchbooks							
Ceremony							
Marriage License							
Site Fee							
Officiant's Fee							
Rentals (chairs, etc.)							
Other							
Other							
Other							
Other							

A Budget You Can Live With

Wedding Expenses Worksheet

	Preliminary Estimate	To Be Paid By	Vendor's Estimate	Deposit Amt.	Date Paid	Balance Due	Date Paid
Reception							
Site Fee							
Food/Caterer							
Beverages							
Cake							
Serving Staff							
Equipment/Rentals							
Rings							
Engagement Ring							
Her Wedding Band							
His Wedding Band							
Flowers							
Ceremony Site							
Bridal Bouquet							
Attendants' Bouquets							
Groom's Boutonniere							
Groomsmen's Boutonnieres							
Corsages							
Reception Site							
Music							
Ceremony							
Reception							
Photography							
Portraits							
Engagement							
Wedding							
Wedding album							
On-Site Services							
Parents' Albums							
Extra Pictures							
Videography							
Other							
Other							

A Budget You Can Live With

Wedding Expenses Worksheet

	Preliminary Estimate	To Be Paid By	Vendor's Estimate	Deposit Amt.	Date Paid	Balance Due	Date Paid
Transportation							
Out-of-Town Guests							
Bride & Groom							
Gifts							
Attendants							
Groomsmen							
Hospitality							
Baskets for Out-of-Town Guests							
Favors							
Other							
Other							
Other							
Parties							
Engagement							
Bride's Luncheon							
Rehearsal Dinner							
Gift-Opening Brunch							
Honeymoon							
Transportation							
Accommodations							
Daily Expenses							
Other Expenses							

A Budget You Can Live With

Invitations, Programs & Announcements

✶ ✶ ✶ ✶ ✶

The Guest List

Negotiating the Number

Wedding guest lists have a tendency to become amorphous blobs if they are not controlled and contained from the get-go. The number of invitees will be influenced by your wedding style, the budget, and space limitations of the ceremony and reception sites. Before gathering lists of potential guests, the bride, the groom, and both sets of parents should discuss their myriad visions of the event. Will children be welcome? Will it be an intimate gathering of a few dozen close friends and family, or a large-scale gala? Define "a few dozen." Define "large scale." Be sure to arrive at an actual number. The total can be split, with the groom's family and the bride's family each inviting half, or it can be divided into thirds among the couple, the groom's family and the bride's family.

Each of these parties compile their own guest list. Be sure to count spouses (or dates) and children. The list should include accurate spellings of names as well as addresses of the people to be invited. If any of the parties has a list that's disproportionately large, they may have to rate the individuals as A-list, B-list, or C-list in order to determine who will make the final cut.

By a preordained deadline, gather together each party's list and store it in a folder you've purchased for all of your receipts, estimates and random lists. But before you do that, check to see that no one's been overly inclusive. Note any duplicates. Be sure that you've included the names of your attendants and yourselves, plus both sets of immediate families. On page 17 you'll begin compiling your Master Guest List.

Along with guest lists, ask both sets of parents and your spouse-to-be for a list of people who should receive announcements. Wedding announcements can be sent to extended family members, distant friends, and anyone who would like to know that you are getting married but who will not be invited to the wedding. It's customary to send out announcements after the ceremony.

No Regrets

Some sources suggest that you can expect 25 percent of the guests to be unable to attend. They further suggest a "guest wish-list"; then, as guests send their regrets, you can turn around and invite those on the wish list. It's acceptable to send invitations up to three weeks before the ceremony. Common sense suggests that this exercise could be a minefield of hurt feelings. Use grace and caution.

Compiling the Master Guest List

Assuming you've gathered guest lists from both sides of the family, you're ready to compile the Master Guest List. Although the computer-savvy bride or groom may feel compelled to create a guest-list databank, it might be a wasted effort if you want the invitations to be formal, in which case the envelopes should be addressed by hand. However, if you will be using the list for Christmas cards or other correspondence in the years to come, go ahead and make that databank. You know you'll feel better.

As you compile the Master Guest List, take into account that some people will bring both dates and children, even if they're not specifically invited. This can cause your guest list to expand exponentially. In terms of etiquette, only those persons named on the invitation are invited, but many people will simply assume you'll welcome the entire family. (If you don't want young children in the chapel, you may want to hire someone to provide childcare in a nearby room during the ceremony.)

Be sure to give a copy of the Master Guest List to the person who will be handling invitation RSVPs—typically the bride or the bride's mother. (A week or so before the wedding, phone calls may have to be made to important people who haven't responded to the invitation. Etiquette suggests that the bride and groom should not be the ones to make these queries. Let the parents of the happy couple be the ones to adopt this task.)

Although most caterers suggest ordering 10 percent more food and drink than your RSVPs dictate, you'll need a fairly accurate head count.

Invitations

Invitations can be works of art, with calligraphy and even paper made by your own hands (or those of a well-paid professional). Depending on your priorities and talents, invitations may be ordered from a print shop or created on a home computer. Before placing an order or creating your own, check with several printers to get ideas about styles of invitations as well as the wording. There are traditional ways of phrasing announcements, which most printers can supply, or you may want to create a contemporary wording that feels better suited to your sensibilities.

Formal embossed invitations should be ordered three months before the wedding. This allows one month for the printer, and two weeks for you to address them by hand. Invitations should be sent four to six weeks before the wedding, sooner if the big day falls on a holiday weekend or if there will be many out-of-town guests who will need time to make travel plans.

You'll want to include a stamped RSVP reply card and a map with directions to the ceremony and reception. Order more invitations than you think you'll need so that you can extend last-minute invitations. Ask the printer if you can get the envelopes right away, so that you and your intended can start addressing them. At the same time you order invitations, order thank-you notes and announcements. Check on prices for place cards, napkins, and other trinkets that you'll want for the reception.

* * * * *

Wording of Invitation

Printers' Estimates

Printer #1
PRICE FOR INVITATIONS
(INCLUDING RESPONSE CARDS, MAPS, ENVELOPES)
PHONE
THANK-YOU NOTES
ANNOUNCEMENTS
PLACE CARDS
NAPKINS
MATCHES

TOTAL COST

Printer #2
PRICE FOR INVITATIONS
(INCLUDING RESPONSE CARDS, MAPS, ENVELOPES)
PHONE
THANK-YOU NOTES
ANNOUNCEMENTS
PLACE CARDS
NAPKINS
MATCHES

TOTAL COST

Printer #3
PRICE FOR INVITATIONS
(INCLUDING RESPONSE CARDS, MAPS, ENVELOPES)
PHONE
THANK-YOU NOTES
ANNOUNCEMENTS
PLACE CARDS
NAPKINS
MATCHES

TOTAL COST

Invitations, Programs & Announcements

* * * * *

Master Guest List

Space for 169 invitees is provided on the following pages. A separate list for announcements is provided later in this chapter

Name
Address

Invitation Sent ☐

Name
Address

Invitation Sent ☐

Name
Address

Invitation Sent ☐

Name
Address

Invitation Sent ☐

Name
Address

Invitation Sent ☐

Name
Address

Invitation Sent ☐

Name
Address

Invitation Sent ☐

Name
Address

Invitation Sent ☐

Name
Address

Invitation Sent ☐

Name
Address

Invitation Sent ☐

Name
Address

Invitation Sent ☐

Name
Address

Invitation Sent ☐

Name
Address

Invitation Sent ☐

Name
Address

Invitation Sent ☐

Name
Address

Invitation Sent ☐

Name
Address

Invitation Sent ☐

Name
Address

Invitation Sent ☐

Invitations, Programs & Announcements

* * * * *

NAME
ADDRESS

INVITATION SENT ☐

NAME
ADDRESS

INVITATION SENT ☐

NAME
ADDRESS

INVITATION SENT ☐

NAME
ADDRESS

INVITATION SENT ☐

NAME
ADDRESS

INVITATION SENT ☐

NAME
ADDRESS

INVITATION SENT ☐

NAME
ADDRESS

INVITATION SENT ☐

NAME
ADDRESS

INVITATION SENT ☐

NAME
ADDRESS

INVITATION SENT ☐

NAME
ADDRESS

INVITATION SENT ☐

NAME
ADDRESS

INVITATION SENT ☐

NAME
ADDRESS

INVITATION SENT ☐

NAME
ADDRESS

INVITATION SENT ☐

NAME
ADDRESS

INVITATION SENT ☐

NAME
ADDRESS

INVITATION SENT ☐

NAME
ADDRESS

INVITATION SENT ☐

NAME
ADDRESS

INVITATION SENT ☐

NAME
ADDRESS

INVITATION SENT ☐

Invitations, Programs & Announcements

★ ★ ★ ★ ★

NAME _____
ADDRESS _____
_____ INVITATION SENT ☐

NAME _____
ADDRESS _____
_____ INVITATION SENT ☐

NAME _____
ADDRESS _____
_____ INVITATION SENT ☐

NAME _____
ADDRESS _____
_____ INVITATION SENT ☐

NAME _____
ADDRESS _____
_____ INVITATION SENT ☐

NAME _____
ADDRESS _____
_____ INVITATION SENT ☐

NAME _____
ADDRESS _____
_____ INVITATION SENT ☐

NAME _____
ADDRESS _____
_____ INVITATION SENT ☐

NAME _____
ADDRESS _____
_____ INVITATION SENT ☐

NAME _____
ADDRESS _____
_____ INVITATION SENT ☐

NAME _____
ADDRESS _____
_____ INVITATION SENT ☐

NAME _____
ADDRESS _____
_____ INVITATION SENT ☐

NAME _____
ADDRESS _____
_____ INVITATION SENT ☐

NAME _____
ADDRESS _____
_____ INVITATION SENT ☐

NAME _____
ADDRESS _____
_____ INVITATION SENT ☐

NAME _____
ADDRESS _____
_____ INVITATION SENT ☐

Invitations, Programs & Announcements

✳ ✳ ✳ ✳

NAME	NAME
ADDRESS	ADDRESS
INVITATION SENT ☐	INVITATION SENT ☐
NAME	NAME
ADDRESS	ADDRESS
INVITATION SENT ☐	INVITATION SENT ☐
NAME	NAME
ADDRESS	ADDRESS
INVITATION SENT ☐	INVITATION SENT ☐
NAME	NAME
ADDRESS	ADDRESS
INVITATION SENT ☐	INVITATION SENT ☐
NAME	NAME
ADDRESS	ADDRESS
INVITATION SENT ☐	INVITATION SENT ☐
NAME	NAME
ADDRESS	ADDRESS
INVITATION SENT ☐	INVITATION SENT ☐
NAME	NAME
ADDRESS	ADDRESS
INVITATION SENT ☐	INVITATION SENT ☐
NAME	NAME
ADDRESS	ADDRESS
INVITATION SENT ☐	INVITATION SENT ☐
NAME	NAME
ADDRESS	ADDRESS
INVITATION SENT ☐	INVITATION SENT ☐

Invitations, Programs & Announcements

* * * * *

Name		Name	
Address		Address	
	Invitation Sent ☐		Invitation Sent ☐
Name		Name	
Address		Address	
	Invitation Sent ☐		Invitation Sent ☐
Name		Name	
Address		Address	
	Invitation Sent ☐		Invitation Sent ☐
Name		Name	
Address		Address	
	Invitation Sent ☐		Invitation Sent ☐
Name		Name	
Address		Address	
	Invitation Sent ☐		Invitation Sent ☐
Name		Name	
Address		Address	
	Invitation Sent ☐		Invitation Sent ☐
Name		Name	
Address		Address	
	Invitation Sent ☐		Invitation Sent
Name		Name	
Address		Address	
	Invitation Sent ☐		Invitation S
Name		Name	
Address		Address	
	Invitation Sent ☐		Invitation
Name		Name	
Address		Address	
	Invitation Sent ☐		Invitation

Invitations, Programs & Announcements

* * * * *

Name
Address

                    Invitation Sent ☐

Name
Address

                    Invitation Sent ☐

Name
Address

                    Invitation Sent ☐

Name
Address

                    Invitation Sent ☐

Name
Address

                    Invitation Sent ☐

Name
Address

                    Invitation Sent ☐

Name
Address

                    Invitation Sent ☐

Name
Address

                    Invitation Sent ☐

Name
Address

                    Invitation Sent ☐

Name
Address

                    Invitation Sent ☐

Name
Address

                    Invitation Sent ☐

Name
Address

                    Invitation Sent ☐

Name
Address

                    Invitation Sent ☐

Name
Address

                    Invitation Sent ☐

Name
Address

                    Invitation Sent ☐

Name
Address

                    Invitation Sent ☐

Name
Address

                    Invitation Sent ☐

Name
Address

                    Invitation Sent ☐

Invitations, Programs & Announcements

* * * *

NAME	NAME
ADDRESS	ADDRESS
INVITATION SENT ☐	INVITATION SENT ☐
NAME	NAME
ADDRESS	ADDRESS
INVITATION SENT ☐	INVITATION SENT ☐
NAME	NAME
ADDRESS	ADDRESS
INVITATION SENT ☐	INVITATION SENT ☐
NAME	NAME
ADDRESS	ADDRESS
INVITATION SENT ☐	INVITATION SENT ☐
NAME	NAME
ADDRESS	ADDRESS
INVITATION SENT ☐	INVITATION SENT ☐
NAME	NAME
ADDRESS	ADDRESS
INVITATION SENT ☐	INVITATION SENT ☐
NAME	NAME
ADDRESS	ADDRESS
INVITATION SENT ☐	INVITATION SENT ☐
NAME	NAME
ADDRESS	ADDRESS
INVITATION SENT ☐	INVITATION SENT ☐
NAME	NAME
ADDRESS	ADDRESS
INVITATION SENT ☐	INVITATION SENT ☐

Invitations, Programs & Announcements

* * * * *

Name		Name	
Address		Address	
	Invitation Sent ☐		Invitation Sent ☐
Name		Name	
Address		Address	
	Invitation Sent ☐		Invitation Sent ☐
Name		Name	
Address		Address	
	Invitation Sent ☐		Invitation Sent ☐
Name		Name	
Address		Address	
	Invitation Sent ☐		Invitation Sent ☐
Name		Name	
Address		Address	
	Invitation Sent ☐		Invitation Sent ☐
Name		Name	
Address		Address	
	Invitation Sent ☐		Invitation Sent ☐
Name		Name	
Address		Address	
	Invitation Sent ☐		Invitation Sent ☐
Name		Name	
Address		Address	
	Invitation Sent ☐		Invitation Sent ☐
Name		Name	
Address		Address	
	Invitation Sent ☐		Invitation Sent ☐

Invitations, Programs & Announcements

* * * * *

Thank-You Notes

While you're at the printer, you should consider ordering thank-you notes imprinted with your names—something in keeping with the style of your invitations and announcements. Plain cards, available from any department store, are perfectly acceptable. The important thing is that you have them on hand so that you can write the notes as you receive the gifts. Each note should be sent within a few weeks of receiving the gift.

 Thank-you notes should be handwritten by either the bride or the groom. They should mention the gift by name. ("Thanks for the lovely gift," sounds insincere. Instead try, "Thanks for the lovely blue cotton comforter. It will look right at home on our new pine bed." The latter example is not only heartfelt, it has the added benefit of taking up more space on the note card.) If you're sharing the task—which is the only fair way to do it, since the gift is intended for the two of you—be careful to keep track of who is thanking whom. (Later in the planner is a place for listing gifts received and recording thank-you notes sent.)

Name _____
Address _____
       Invitation Sent ☐

Name _____
Address _____
       Invitation Sent ☐

Name _____
Address _____
       Invitation Sent ☐

Name _____
Address _____
       Invitation Sent ☐

Name _____
Address _____
       Invitation Sent ☐

Name _____
Address _____
       Invitation Sent ☐

Name _____
Address _____
       Invitation Sent ☐

Name _____
Address _____
       Invitation Sent ☐

Name _____
Address _____
       Invitation Sent ☐

Wedding Programs

As guests arrive for your ceremony, many will appreciate a wedding program. While some well-wishers will turn directly to the program's schedule of events either to see if any favorite hymns will be sung or to ascertain how long the ceremony will last, other guests are in search of more interesting data concerning you and your wedding party. For instance, a woman in the latter category might say to a spouse in the former category, "Oh, how nice. It says here that Best Man Andrew Forester has been the groom's closest buddy since they attended the Uptown Montessori School …" Some of your guests would love to know that the bride's dress is an heirloom worn by three generations of mothers and daughters. The program is also an ideal place to feature a short memoir of your courtship or a brief note of thanks to your families for their help and support.

The program can be ordered from a printer or created on your home computer. If you don't have examples from past weddings you've attended, ask your printer for prototypes.

Wording of Program

✳ ✳ ✳ ✳

Announcements

As mentioned earlier, announcements of your marriage are sent to colleagues, distant relatives, and friends who were not invited to the wedding. This is a time-honored tradition and you should feel no qualms about sending these cards, since the recipient of a wedding announcement is not expected to send a gift.

Wording of Announcement

Announcements can be ordered at the same time as the invitations, but should not be mailed until the day of the ceremony or shortly thereafter. By its phrasing, the announcement informs recipients of the bride's name after marriage. You may want to include an "at-home card," with the address of the home in which the two of you will be residing.

The Announcements List

In the space that follows, record the names and addresses of people to whom you'll be sending announcements. (Space for 46 entries)

Name
Address

Announcement Sent ☐

Name
Address

Announcement Sent ☐

Name
Address

Announcement Sent ☐

Name
Address

Announcement Sent ☐

Name
Address

Announcement Sent ☐

Name
Address

Announcement Sent ☐

Invitations, Programs & Announcements

* * * * *

Name		Name	
Address		Address	
	Announcement Sent ☐		Announcement Sent ☐
Name		Name	
Address		Address	
	Announcement Sent ☐		Announcement Sent ☐
Name		Name	
Address		Address	
	Announcement Sent ☐		Announcement Sent ☐
Name		Name	
Address		Address	
	Announcement Sent ☐		Announcement Sent ☐
Name		Name	
Address		Address	
	Announcement Sent ☐		Announcement Sent ☐
Name		Name	
Address		Address	
	Announcement Sent ☐		Announcement Sent ☐
Name		Name	
Address		Address	
	Announcement Sent ☐		Announcement Sent ☐
Name		Name	
Address		Address	
	Announcement Sent ☐		Announcement Sent ☐
Name		Name	
Address		Address	
	Announcement Sent ☐		Announcement Sent ☐

Invitations, Programs & Announcements

* * * * *

	Announcement Sent ☐
Name	Name
Address	Address
Announcement Sent ☐	Announcement Sent ☐
Name	Name
Address	Address
Announcement Sent ☐	Announcement Sent ☐
Name	Name
Address	Address
Announcement Sent ☐	Announcement Sent ☐
Name	Name
Address	Address
Announcement Sent ☐	Announcement Sent ☐
Name	Name
Address	Address
Announcement Sent ☐	Announcement Sent ☐
Name	Name
Address	Address
Announcement Sent ☐	Announcement Sent ☐
Name	Name
Address	Address
Announcement Sent ☐	Announcement Sent ☐
Name	Name
Address	Address
Announcement Sent ☐	Announcement Sent ☐
Name	Name
Address	Address
Announcement Sent ☐	Announcement Sent ☐
Name	Name
Address	Address

Invitations, Programs & Announcements

Notes

✶✶✶✶

The Ceremony

THE CEREMONY

The Ceremony

✶ ✶ ✶ ✶ ✶

Time and Place

"So, have you set the date?"

On the surface, it's a simple question. But before you can answer it in the affirmative, you'll have to ask some questions of yourselves. It's time to get down to business, make some decisions, and coordinate certain elements of the ceremony and reception. A couple of basic questions will have to be addressed:

I. Who Will Be Officiating? Will it be a religious or a civil ceremony—that is—will it be performed by clergy or by a justice of the peace?

If you'll be married in a church or synagogue, there are several issues that you'll need to discuss with the minister or rabbi. (Remember: most clergy members expect the couples they marry to attend services regularly—before the wedding.) It's important to know whether a pastor has beliefs that might prevent him or her from performing the ceremony. Issues such as interfaith or second marriages should be openly discussed if they apply to your situation—especially if these issues present potential conflicts between you and the clergy. Some churches and synagogues also require premarital counseling.

Whether you want to write your own vows or simply change a few words of the standard contract, be sure to choose an officiant who will allow you to say the vows that are right for you.

II. Where Will You Be Married, and Will The Reception Site Be Available? Your choice of officiant may well determine the site of the wedding ceremony—particularly if you'll be married by your minister or rabbi. There are a thousand other places to speak your vows: a private home or yard, a country club, an inn or hotel, outdoors in the park or zoo, at a lakeside pavilion or gazebo, or aboard a yacht or riverboat.

Setting the Date

Consult with the officiant and the managers of the wedding and reception sites to coordinate a date that works for everyone. Some sites are booked as early as 12 to 18 months in advance, with Saturday evenings being the most popular (and expensive) time for a wedding. If you want to get married sooner and you're finding that Saturdays are booked, consider getting married on a Friday or Sunday. Will the wedding take place in the morning, afternoon, or evening? Obviously, when you reserve the date, you'll need to reserve the time as well.

* * * * *

Using the calendar as a guide, note potential wedding dates below.

OFFICIANT AVAILABLE:

_____

_____

CEREMONY SITE AVAILABLE:

_____

_____

RECEPTION SITE AVAILABLE:

_____

_____

OUR WEDDING DATE & TIME:

_____

Following is a place to list those chosen to be your "Honored Attendants":

MAID OR MATRON OF HONOR ("BEST WOMAN")

_____

BRIDESMAIDS

_____

_____

_____

_____

_____

BEST MAN

_____

GROOMSMEN

_____

_____

_____

_____

_____

Choosing Your Wedding Party

The number of people in the wedding party is up to you—each half of the couple might have one close friend acting as "Best Man" and "Best Woman," or you could enlist an entourage of eight or ten.

 Traditionally, attendants are expected to pay for their own wedding attire. However, if you know that your kid sister can't afford to buy a dress, you might want to offer to cover the expense. A volunteer seamstress can ease the financial burden as well. Discuss costs when you first ask people to be members of the wedding party.

USHERS (1 FOR EVERY 50 GUESTS)

_____

_____

_____

The Ceremony

* * * * *

The Vows

He Said, She Said

Many officiants, be they clergy or judge, consider the task of marrying people to be the best part of their job. They put great effort into writing eloquent sermons or speeches for the occasion. Work with the officiant to create the wording that best expresses your commitment. You don't have to be a great writer in order to personalize your vows—draw upon the wisdom of the ages by selecting a reading that's meaningful to you.

Wedding Vows

The Ceremony

* * * * *

Site Planning and Decor

The church or synagogue may be able to supply an aisle runner, candelabras, or other items that you want to include in the ceremony, but it's likely you'll have to rent some "extras" to decorate the site.

If you've always dreamed of getting married outdoors, provide yourself with a bit of rain insurance by reserving an indoor space as a back-up or by renting a canopy or a tent. An outdoor setting can be decorated with flowers and ivy, tiki lamps and twinkle lights, trellises and archways. An outdoor "aisle" is easily created by the placement of chairs.

Flowers and music are covered in detail later in the planner.

Below is space for listing decorative items and equipment that you'll need to rent or buy for the ceremony. This might include chairs, canopies, candleholders and lamps, pillows for the rings, or a wine glass (for the "Sharing of the Cup," symbolic of your commitment to share the cup of life; or for stomping on at the end of the ceremony, a Jewish tradition).

Decorative Items & Equipment

The Ceremony

* * * * *

Other Elements

✻ Consider incorporating traditions that are meaningful to you: jumping the broom, lighting a unity candle, or sharing the cup, to name just a few. To learn more about ethnic or religious wedding traditions, take a trip to your local library. *Wild Geese and Tea,* by Shu Shu Costa, details Asian customs, while *Jumping the Broom,* by Harriette Cole, addresses African-American bridal rituals. Several other general wedding guides offer basic information regarding Jewish weddings.

✻ Instead of throwing rice, which is said to be unsafe for birds and is restricted at some locations, there is a growing trend to blow bubbles or toss rose petals or birdseed at the newlywed couple.

✻ Don't forget practical matters. Are there dressing rooms at the ceremony site? Will there be ample parking for guests?

Don't Forget To Bring

✻ The rings
✻ Payments for the officiant and vendors (usually delivered by the Best Man)
✻ Programs for guests
✻ Vows and selected readings
✻ Guest book
✻ Decorating elements and equipment
✻ "Emergency" kit containing aspirin, tissues, safety pins, needle and thread, clear nail polish, tampons
✻ Wedding Planner
✻ Marriage license

Notes

_____
_____
_____
_____
_____
_____
_____

The Ceremony

* * * *

Ceremony Timetable

At the rehearsal, hand out copies of this timetable to all members of the wedding. Be sure that the florist, caterer, and baker receive copies as well.

_____ Photographer arrives

_____ Florist arrives

_____ Ushers arrive
(one half-hour prior to ceremony, earlier for a large wedding)

_____ Musicians arrive

_____ Processional

Order of Processional

_____

_____

_____

_____

_____ Ceremony

_____ Recessional

Order of Recessional

_____

_____

_____

_____ Photo session

Profile: Tammie & Nathan's "Weekend Wedding"

A recent trend in nuptial celebrations is the weekend wedding, where families gather at a resort, bed-and-breakfast, or spa for several days of festivities. Tammie Hudnall and Nathan Koeshall secretly eloped in May a couple of springs ago. For their two-year anniversary, they decided to repeat their vows in front of 75 guests during a weekend wedding celebration at a picturesque lakeshore resort.

As guests arrived on Friday night, they were treated to a get-acquainted barbecue. On Saturday, everyone helped out where they could—in the kitchen, setting up for the ceremony, and placing luminaries along all the footpaths. That afternoon, the couple spoke their vows on a hill overlooking the lake. Children handed each guest a tulip, and each guest in turn gave the flower to Tammie and Nathan, along with a few words, a poem, or a blessing to symbolize their support of the marriage. Afterward, there was dancing at a party in the resort's boat house. On Sunday morning, Tammie and Nathan made breakfast for everyone in their log cabin.

A weekend wedding is perfect for big families who are sprawled across the country, because such a celebration provides an opportunity to slow down and spend time together. Some wedding parties take up residence at a spa or resort a day or two before the wedding, as an antidote to the stress of marriage preparations.

The Reception

The Reception

The Reception

* * * * *

Selecting a Site

The traditional wedding format has the reception following the ceremony, with the guests migrating from one location to the other. In such a case, the choice of reception site will be a factor in setting your wedding date—specifically, whether it's available on the day of the wedding.

Receptions can be held almost anywhere, indoors or out. But whatever site you choose should have an ambiance that's in keeping with the mood and style of the ceremony. Of course, it also must be able to accommodate the number of guests you plan to invite.

Elements of Style

When it comes to planning a wedding, think in terms of style. Style can be created with lighting, color, and other elements that enhance the existing architecture or landscape of your ceremony and reception sites. To achieve a consistency of style throughout the day, first decide on the degree of formality you want. A "very formal" wedding is usually an evening affair. The ceremony takes place in a house of worship and the reception revolves around an extravagant dinner, and thus should be held in a place that can accommodate that. Although a "formal" or "semi-formal" wedding may include some of the same elements as a very formal affair, these ceremonies need not take place in a church or synagogue, and the reception sites do not necessarily require a banquet facility. An "informal" wedding might be held outside in a garden, with tea-length dresses and light refreshments. (These are very general guidelines. Keep in mind that it's possible to have an informal wedding that includes dinner for 150 guests, in which case you might have to coordinate the needs of an off-site caterer with the facilities of the reception site.)

Obviously, food and drink are key elements of the reception, and you may want to consider the less-obvious options. A brunch or luncheon buffet could follow a morning ceremony, or you could celebrate your marriage with an afternoon tea or cocktail party. A very formal evening reception includes dinner, which may be served buffet-style or as a formal sit-down dinner with everything from a cocktail hour to cake and cappuccino.

You'll also want to consider what kind of music will be performed at the reception. Will there be a five-piece ensemble? A jazz band? A D.J. overseeing a laser-light show? Whatever your choice, make sure that the reception hall can accommodate it acoustically, that its electrical system can supply enough power, and that there's ample space for dancing.

Once you've determined what you're looking for, you'll want to visit several places. Then, in the following pages, record information that will help you choose the perfect site for your wedding celebration.

* * * * *

Reception Site # 1

Name
_____

Phone
_____

Contact
_____

Number of guests site
is able to accommodate _____

On-site Catering? ☐ yes ☐ no

If yes, notes regarding menu and cost:
_____
_____
_____
_____
_____
_____

☐ Deposit required? By date _____

Tables, chairs, linens and dinnerware included? ☐ yes ☐ no

If no on-site catering, are there kitchen facilities for the caterer? ☐ yes ☐ no

Adult Beverages

What's available:
_____

Cost or corking fees:
_____

Cake-Baking? ☐ yes ☐ no

If yes, styles available:
_____
_____
_____
_____
_____
_____

Cost _____

Cake-cutting service? ☐ yes ☐ no

Music & Dancing

Can their power supply handle the band or light show? ☐ yes ☐ no

Would the acoustics be right for the music? ☐ yes ☐ no

Is there a dance floor? ☐ yes ☐ no

Total Estimated Cost
including tax and gratuities

_____

Deposit required _____

By date _____

The Reception

* * * * *

Reception Site # 2

Name
_____

Phone
_____

Contact
_____

Number of guests site
is able to accommodate _____

On-site Catering? ☐ yes ☐ no

If yes, notes regarding menu and cost:
_____
_____
_____
_____
_____
_____

☐ Deposit required? By date _____

Tables, chairs, linens and dinnerware included? ☐ yes ☐ no
If no on-site catering, are there kitchen facilities for the caterer? ☐ yes ☐ no

Adult Beverages

What's available:
_____

Cost or corking fees:
_____

Cake-Baking? ☐ yes ☐ no

If yes, styles available:
_____
_____
_____
_____
_____
_____
_____
_____

Cost _____

Cake-cutting service? ☐ yes ☐ no

Music & Dancing

Can their power supply handle the band or light show? ☐ yes ☐ no

Would the acoustics be right for the music? ☐ yes ☐ no

Is there a dance floor? ☐ yes ☐ no

Total Estimated Cost
including tax and gratuities
_____

Deposit required _____

By date _____

The Reception

* * * * *

Reception Site # 3

Name
_____

Phone
_____

Contact
_____

Number of guests site
is able to accommodate _____

On-site Catering? ☐ yes ☐ no

If yes, notes regarding menu and cost:
_____
_____
_____
_____
_____
_____

☐ Deposit required? By date _____

Tables, chairs, linens and dinnerware included? ☐ yes ☐ no

If no on-site catering, are there kitchen facilities for the caterer? ☐ yes ☐ no

Adult Beverages

What's available:
_____

Cost or corking fees:
_____

Cake-Baking? ☐ yes ☐ no

If yes, styles available:
_____
_____
_____
_____
_____
_____
_____

Cost _____

Cake-cutting service? ☐ yes ☐ no

Music & Dancing

Can their power supply handle the band or light show? ☐ yes ☐ no

Would the acoustics be right for the music? ☐ yes ☐ no

Is there a dance floor? ☐ yes ☐ no

Total Estimated Cost

including tax and gratuities
_____

Deposit required _____

By date _____

The Reception

* * * * *

Reception Site # 4

Name
_____

Phone
_____

Contact
_____

Number of guests site
is able to accommodate _____

On-site Catering? ☐ yes ☐ no

If yes, notes regarding menu and cost:
_____
_____
_____
_____
_____
_____

☐ Deposit required? By date _____

Tables, chairs, linens and dinnerware included? ☐ yes ☐ no
If no on-site catering, are there kitchen facilities for the caterer? ☐ yes ☐ no

Adult Beverages

What's available:
_____

Cost or corking fees:
_____

Cake-Baking? ☐ yes ☐ no

If yes, styles available:
_____
_____
_____
_____
_____
_____

Cost _____

Cake-cutting service? ☐ yes ☐ no

Music & Dancing

Can their power supply handle the band or light show? ☐ yes ☐ no

Would the acoustics be right for the music? ☐ yes ☐ no

Is there a dance floor? ☐ yes ☐ no

Total Estimated Cost
including tax and gratuities
_____

Deposit required _____

By date _____

The Reception

* * * * *

Catering

Many sites offer in-house catering services. With some, you'll have no choice but to use their services. However, receptions that take place outdoors, at a private home, or in a civic or historic building may require the services of an independent caterer. The general vicinity is home to dozens of such businesses, from individuals who lovingly create out of their own kitchens to well-known chefs who oversee gourmet restaurants and legions of slicers, dicers, sauce-makers and cake-bakers. If you're unfamiliar with a caterer's work, ask to sample his or her wares.

Food & Beverages

_____
_____
_____
_____
_____
_____
_____
_____
_____
_____
_____
_____

Caterer #1

Name
_____
Phone
_____
Contact
_____

Menu Options

Meal type
☐ brunch ☐ lunch
☐ hors d'oeuvres only ☐ dinner

Buffet
_____
_____
_____

Sit-Down
_____
_____
_____

Beverages & Food

☐ wine ☐ champagne ☐ open bar
☐ espresso bar ☐ punch ☐ tea

Food servers &
bartenders included? ☐ yes ☐ no

Require on-site kitchen? ☐ yes ☐ no

Serving dishes, dinnerware &
flatware included? ☐ yes ☐ no

Cost of food & drink per guest _____
Final headcount needed by date _____

Total Estimated Cost

including tax and gratuities _____

Deposit required _____

By date _____

The Reception

* * * * *

Caterer #2

Name
_____

Phone
_____

Contact
_____

Menu Options

Meal type
☐ brunch ☐ lunch
☐ hors d'oeuvres only ☐ dinner

Buffet
_____
_____
_____

Sit-Down
_____
_____
_____

Beverages & Food
☐ wine ☐ champagne ☐ open bar
☐ espresso bar ☐ punch ☐ tea

Food servers &
bartenders included? ☐ yes ☐ no

Require on-site kitchen? ☐ yes ☐ no

Serving dishes, dinnerware &
flatware included? ☐ yes ☐ no

Cost of food & drink per guest _____
Final headcount needed by date _____

Total Estimated Cost
including tax and gratuities _____

Deposit required _____

By date _____

Caterer #3

Name
_____

Phone
_____

Contact
_____

Menu Options

Meal type
☐ brunch ☐ lunch
☐ hors d'oeuvres only ☐ dinner

Buffet
_____
_____
_____

Sit-Down
_____
_____
_____

Beverages & Food
☐ wine ☐ champagne ☐ open bar
☐ espresso bar ☐ punch ☐ tea

Food servers &
bartenders included? ☐ yes ☐ no

Require on-site kitchen? ☐ yes ☐ no

Serving dishes, dinnerware &
flatware included? ☐ yes ☐ no

Cost of food & drink per guest _____
Final headcount needed by date _____

Total Estimated Cost
including tax and gratuities _____

Deposit required _____

By date _____

The Reception

* * * * *

Caterer #4

Name _____

Phone _____

Contact _____

Menu Options

Meal type
☐ brunch ☐ lunch
☐ hors d'oeuvres only ☐ dinner

Buffet _____
_____
_____

Sit-Down _____
_____
_____

Beverages & Food
☐ wine ☐ champagne ☐ open bar
☐ espresso bar ☐ punch ☐ tea

Food servers &
bartenders included? ☐ yes ☐ no

Require on-site kitchen? ☐ yes ☐ no

Serving dishes, dinnerware &
flatware included? ☐ yes ☐ no

Cost of food & drink per guest _____
Final headcount needed by date _____

Total Estimated Cost
including tax and gratuities _____

Deposit required _____

By date _____

Caterer #5

Name _____

Phone _____

Contact _____

Menu Options

Meal type
☐ brunch ☐ lunch
☐ hors d'oeuvres only ☐ dinner

Buffet _____
_____
_____

Sit-Down _____
_____
_____

Beverages & Food
☐ wine ☐ champagne ☐ open bar
☐ espresso bar ☐ punch ☐ tea

Food servers &
bartenders included? ☐ yes ☐ no

Require on-site kitchen? ☐ yes ☐ no

Serving dishes, dinnerware &
flatware included? ☐ yes ☐ no

Cost of food & drink per guest _____
Final headcount needed by date _____

Total Estimated Cost
including tax and gratuities _____

Deposit required _____

By date _____

The Reception

* * * * *

The Wedding Cake

Although some reception sites and caterers can also supply your wedding cake, remember that cake-baking is an art unto itself. Therefore, you may want to consider hiring a baker who will bring all of his or her talents to bear. Wedding cakes need not be white towers of iced confection topped with a miniature bride and groom (although if that's your heart's desire, you surely will be able to find a vendor who can create it). Take into account your favorite flavors, and ask bakers what they consider to be their specialty. Today's cakes can be decorated with sugared berries, white chocolate rosebuds, ribbons of ganache or fresh flowers. The cake should be ordered at least eight weeks before the wedding. As you shop for a baker, ask the following questions:

Baker #1

Name
_____

Phone
_____

Style & Flavor Options
_____
_____
_____

Cake-Cutting Service? ☐ yes ☐ no

Total Cost _____

Deposit required _____
By date _____

Delivery or Pick-Up Date & Time

Baker #2

Name
_____

Phone
_____

Style & Flavor Options
_____
_____
_____

Cake-Cutting Service? ☐ yes ☐ no

Total Cost _____

Deposit required _____
By date _____

Delivery or Pick-Up Date & Time

Baker #3

Name
_____

Phone
_____

Style & Flavor Options
_____
_____
_____

Cake-Cutting Service? ☐ yes ☐ no

Total Cost _____

Deposit required _____
By date _____

Delivery or Pick-Up Date & Time

The Reception

* * * * *

Reception Decor

The existing architecture and decor of your reception site can be enhanced with floral arrangements, special lighting, and splashes of color. Choose flowers and table linens that complement the bridal party's attire or the overall wedding style.

Your guests may be spending a great deal of time sitting at their tables, so set these tables with care. Choose centerpieces that won't get in the way of conversation, and consider your tableware options. Will the plates be Spode china or Chinet in rattan holders? Real silverware or plastic forks? Cloth napkins or paper? Naturally, your choices will vary depending on the formality of the event and what your reception site provides.

In addition to a centerpiece, you may want to include some other wedding goodies on the table, such as calligraphied menus or placecards, disposable cameras, and special keepsakes or favors.

Items to be Rented or Purchased

	Source	Price	Reserved/Purchased
Tables			
Chairs			
Slipcovers			
Dance Floor			
Canopy/Tent			
Generator			
Candles			
Candleholders			
Linens			
Trays			
Serving Dishes			
Dinnerware			
Glassware			
Flatware			
Other			
Other			
Other			
Other			
Other			
Other			
Other			
Other			

Reception Timetable

So that the events of the reception move along smoothly, put together a timetable and make sure that the caterer, head musician, and the photographer receive a copy. This is only a sample timetable. Your reception will undoubtedly involve different elements in a different order.

_____ Receiving Line

_____ Cocktail Hour

_____ Guests Take Their Seats for Dinner

_____ Cake

_____ Dancing

First Dance _____

Second Dance _____

_____ Tossing of Bouquet

_____ Couple Departs

Profile: Tim & Teresa's Hand-made Wedding

Teresa Pearson and Tim Cook were married in the summer on the courthouse steps in a small town. The train of Teresa's gown, dotted with silk rosebuds, cascaded down the stairs. Tim had even shed his dreadlocks in favor of more conservative look. He'd built both the arbor under which he and Teresa were wed, as well as a podium from which the judge performed the service. After the ceremony, guests wandered about the historic building, where the judge's podium now served as a holder for the guest book. Next to that was a white mailbox—which Teresa had adorned with the couple's names and stenciled with ivy—serving as a place for guests to drop off cards. There was laughter and champagne, and the party drifted up the ribboned staircase for dinner. Guests chose their places at tables decorated with brightly colored Victorian runners and coordinating cloth napkins. Each napkin was rolled inside a small grapevine wreath of dried flowers. Birdseed-filled tulle bags tied with ribbon were placed next to each place setting for tossing at the bride and groom upon their departure.

The effect was impressive, and such custom-made items are not very costly, according to Teresa. "If you have a little time or a really great group of friends—and a couple of hot glue guns," she adds, "it's not that expensive." The grapevine wreaths cost about five cents each at a craft-supply store; the dried flowers cost about 30 cents a bag. Teresa bought yards and yards of tulle for the elegant bags of birdseed.

At home with Tim afterward, Teresa glances down at the runner that was used at her own wedding table. She remembers the hours spent wrapping embroidery thread around her forefingers to make the tassels for each runner. Outside, Tim's wedding arbor now stands in the yard, covered with flowers. The ivy-covered mailbox is at the end of the driveway, serving its intended purpose. Teresa and Tim see their handiwork beyond their own garden walk; at the homes of friends, Teresa's tiny grapevine wreaths hold tapered candles and are charming reminders of a beautiful wedding.

Notes

* * * *

Wedding Attire

WEDDING ATTIRE

✻

THE RINGS

Wedding Attire

✶ ✶ ✶ ✶ ✶

Getting Dressed

As with every other aspect of the wedding day, there's a traditional way of dressing the bride, the groom, and their attendants. But who says you have to follow tradition? Although many women dream of walking down the aisle in a white wedding gown with a 20-foot train, a flowing veil and white gloves, others see themselves in a simple, tea-length dress with a wreath of flowers in their hair. And some brides completely buck tradition and slink into a berry-colored sheath or a black slipdress.

For grooms, there's a long-standing tradition of tuxedo rental: The black tie and tails, striped vest or cummerbund—or some variation thereof. But there's no reason a man can't have a suit custom-made for the occasion. What's good for the bride is good for the groom. Picture it—a trim new suit in charcoal gray or black, a white shirt with a banded collar.

When it comes to clothing the wedding party, from the bride and groom to the attendants and the couple's parents, the important thing is that there's a harmony of color and style. What style? That depends on the level of formality, the season, and the location of your wedding. Don't be shy. If ever you needed an excuse to dress dramatically, this is it.

Bridal Attire

There are many different paths to your ideal dress. The most obvious would be a bridal salon, but you can also shop consignment stores, wholesale factory outlets, and antique shops. In recent years, a few formalwear stores have started to offer wedding dress rentals. Wearing your mother's or your grandmother's wedding gown is another possibility, or you may have your wedding dress custom-made. The seamstress could be a professional, a friend or family member who volunteers the work, or yourself.

A traditional wedding gown and veil can cost anywhere from $300 to $3,000 or more, depending on the store and designer. A dress may be custom-made for much less (or much more). To get an idea of current styles and trends, look through recent issues of bridal magazines. Many suggest that you start shopping for a dress nine months before the wedding so that you can order six months in advance. If you decide to use the services of a bridal salon, be sure to select a reputable store with a salesperson who understands your tastes and respects your budget. Ask about the amount required for a deposit (50 percent is standard), and the store's policies regarding alterations and fees, number of fittings, and exchanges and cancellations.

When you shop for your dress, bring along your mother, a friend, or even your fiancé. Don't forget to bring pictures from magazines, and a strapless bra for

✳ ✳ ✳ ✳

trying on dresses. Whether you're borrowing a gown, buying one new or old, renting, or having a dress sewn just for you, you can use the following worksheets to record the details.

Something Old

Chalk it up to nostalgia or thrift, but there's been a surge in the popularity of antique wedding dresses, particularly in flapper styles from the era of Scott and Zelda. Even the groom may want to search the recesses of Grandfather's trunk or a local second-hand shop. Although retro suits and dresses may have to be torn apart and completely reconstructed in order to fit the modern-day groom and bride, the clothing also offers a uniqueness of style that can't be found off-the-rack.

Bridal Dress #1

Color

Designer

Style #

Source

Contact

Cost of Alterations or Seamstress

Cost of Fabric & Materials

Rental Fee or Purchase Price

Bridal Dress #2

Color

Designer

Style #

Source

Contact

Cost of Alterations or Seamstress

Cost of Fabric & Materials

Rental Fee or Purchase Price

Bridal Dress #3

Color

Designer

Style #

Source

Contact

Cost of Alterations or Seamstress

Cost of Fabric & Materials

Rental Fee or Purchase Price

Wedding Attire

* * * * *

Bridal Dress #4

Color

Designer

Style #

Source

Contact

Cost of Alterations or Seamstress

Cost of Fabric & Materials

Rental Fee or Purchase Price

Bridal Dress #5

Color

Designer

Style #

Source

Contact

Cost of Alterations or Seamstress

Cost of Fabric & Materials

Rental fee or Purchase Price

Bride's Attire

	Manufacturer & Style Number	Source	Delivery Date	Cost	Deposit	Balance Due
Wedding Attire						
Gown						
Veil or Headpiece						
Shoes						
Hosiery						
Slip						
Bra						
Gloves						
Jewelry						
Garter						
Other						
Other						
Other						
Other						
Other						

Wedding Attire

* * * * *

Bridal Attendants

The scene: The closet of any woman who has been a bridesmaid more than once. From the recesses of her closet, our heroine pulls out something that looks like it's made of upholstery fabric. It's got sleeves—sleeves that were apparently inspired by Imelda Marcos. Our heroine holds up the dress so that her friend can get a closer look. The friend gingerly touches the fabric and then explodes into raucous laughter. Our heroine has to laugh, too, although the amount she paid for this dress is not funny, not funny at all. "Have you ever seen anything so hideous?" she asks through her laughter and tears. "And the bride was convinced this was something I could wear again and again!" More raucous laughter, and fade out.

It's the eternal lament of bridesmaids everywhere. Even a bride who has impeccable taste can become the monster behind this tale. Because it doesn't matter if the dress is made out of chintz or silk, has a lovely portrait collar or a big pink bow on the back—if the bridesmaids are not consulted, at least one of them will consider it the ugliest thing she has ever seen in her life. (Particularly if she has to dole out several hundred dollars for the pleasure of wearing it.)

The way to prevent this is to gather your attendants together to look through magazines and discuss likes and dislikes. In the end, it's the bride who sets the style of the wedding party, but a sensitive bride will respect her attendants' feelings. This is also a good time to gather information about sizes, because while you want to be respectful of your attendants' opinions, you don't want all of them present when you're shopping for dresses. Ask just one attendant, your maid or matron of honor, to accompany you.

You can shop for bridesmaids dresses at the bridal salon, have them custom-made, or buy them off-the-rack.

Record attendants' sizes in the chart below.

Maid/Matron of Honor

Dress Size _____

Bust _____ Waist _____ Hips _____

Shoe Size _____ Glove Size _____

color or style she is *not* comfortable wearing
_____
_____

Bridesmaid #1

Dress Size _____

Bust _____ Waist _____ Hips _____

Shoe Size _____ Glove Size _____

color or style she is *not* comfortable wearing
_____
_____

* * * * *

Bridesmaid #2

DRESS SIZE

BUST   WAIST   HIPS

SHOE SIZE   GLOVE SIZE

COLOR OR STYLE SHE IS *not* COMFORTABLE WEARING

Bridesmaid #3

DRESS SIZE

BUST   WAIST   HIPS

SHOE SIZE   GLOVE SIZE

COLOR OR STYLE SHE IS *not* COMFORTABLE WEARING

Bridesmaid #4

DRESS SIZE

BUST   WAIST   HIPS

SHOE SIZE   GLOVE SIZE

COLOR OR STYLE SHE IS *not* COMFORTABLE WEARING

Bridesmaid #5

DRESS SIZE

BUST   WAIST   HIPS

SHOE SIZE   GLOVE SIZE

COLOR OR STYLE SHE IS *not* COMFORTABLE WEARING

Dress Options for Attendants

MAID/MATRON OF HONOR

Option #1

SOURCE

CONTACT

PHONE NUMBER

COST OF ALTERATIONS OR SEAMSTRESS

RENTAL FEE OR PURCHASE PRICE

COST OF FABRIC & MATERIALS

<u>Wedding Attire</u>

* * * * *

Maid/Matron of Honor, cont.

Option #2

_____

_____

Source _____

Contact _____

Phone Number _____

Cost of Alterations or Seamstress ___

Rental Fee or Purchase Price ___

Cost of Fabric & Materials ___

_____

Option #3

_____

_____

Source _____

Contact _____

Phone Number _____

Cost of Alterations or Seamstress ___

Rental Fee or Purchase Price ___

Cost of Fabric & Materials ___

Bridesmaids

Option #1

_____

_____

Source _____

Contact _____

Phone Number _____

Cost of Alterations or Seamstress ___

Rental Fee or Purchase Price ___

Cost of Fabric & Materials ___

_____

Option #2

_____

_____

Source _____

Contact _____

Phone Number _____

Cost of Alterations or Seamstress ___

Rental Fee or Purchase Price ___

Cost of Fabric & Materials ___

Wedding Attire

* * * * *

Option #3

Source

Contact

Phone Number

Cost of Alterations or Seamstress

Rental Fee or Purchase Price

Cost of Fabric & Materials

Option #4

Source

Contact

Phone Number

Cost of Alterations or Seamstress

Rental Fee or Purchase Price

Cost of Fabric & Materials

Attendants' Dresses

	Description (or Pattern Number)	Size	Source	Fitting Date	Delivery Date	Cost
Maid or Matron of Honor						
Bridesmaids						
Accessories						
Shoes						
Hosiery						
Slip						
Bra						
Gloves						
Jewelry						
Other						
Flower Girl						

Wedding Attire

* * * * *

Flower Girl

The flower girl may wear a dress that is short or floor-length. It's often white to match the bride (some wedding gowns have matching dresses for the flower girl), but a variance of colors and styles is acceptable. Your smallest attendant can carry a bouquet, a basket of flowers flowing with ribbons, or wear a wreath of flowers in her hair.

The Mothers

Traditionally, the mother of the bride chooses her dress before the mother of the groom chooses hers. Their dresses should be in harmony with the style of the wedding.

Groom's Attire

"How does the groom find out which way the current is flowing? Do not ask your father, unless you want to wear something six years out of date. Do not go on your own instincts, unless you want to wear something that looks like it came off The Love Boat *(the source of many half-baked notions about romance and formal wear). An excellent source of insider information about current fashion is that stack of magazines that your fiancée has accumulated, all of which have the word Bride in the title." — from* The Groom's Survival Manual *by Michael R. Perry (Pocket Books, 1991).*

Even if your intended doesn't own a tie—perhaps especially if he doesn't own a tie—he may be surprised at the thrill of donning his wedding suit. As with most matters of the heart, he should consider every option, whether it's an antique store for a vintage suit, a tailor for one that's custom-made, or the local mall for the ubiquitous tuxedo rental.

According to a representative of one formalwear chain, black continues to be the most-favored tuxedo color. Formal vests—lately featuring paisley or black-on-black textured patterns, jewel tones or even muted pastels—have overtaken the cummerbund in popularity. (Any guy working at a tuxedo shop or men's store should be able to show actual examples of "muted pastels" as well as "jewel tones," which until now the average guy may have known as "light pink" and "emerald green." Just for fun and to test the hipness of your local shopkeeper, ask to see something in "eggplant" or "seafoam.")

The groom should choose a white or off-white shirt that complements your wedding gown. Depending on the style of the shirt, a groom may wear a traditional bow tie, the new "Euro-band tie" (a cross between a bow tie and a necktie), or a dramatic silk ascot. For a different look, he might try a banded or mandarin collar, accented with a silk-covered button or jeweled stud. If the groom wants to wear less-formal attire, make sure that the style and colors complement your own look.

* * * * *

Groom's Attire

Option #1

Manufacturer

Style

Color   Size

Source

Contact   Phone

Cost of Alterations or Tailor

Cost of Fabric & Materials

Rental Fee or Purchase Price

Option #2

Manufacturer

Style

Color   Size

Source

Contact   Phone

Cost of Alterations or Tailor

Cost of Fabric & Materials

Rental Fee or Purchase Price

Groom's Attire

	Source	Cost	Deposit	Balance Due
If buying a suit or having one made				
If renting a tuxedo				
Accessories Shoes Socks Hat Gloves Other Other Other Other				

Wedding Attire

* * * * *

Groom's Attendants

The best man, groomsmen, and ushers may be outfitted in suits or tuxedos that coordinate with the groom's attire. If the groom is wearing a double-breasted tuxedo, his groomsmen could wear a single-breasted version. If the men will be wearing their own suits, the colors should be uniform—for instance, everyone in black or in gray tones.

If you'll be renting tuxedos, you'll need to know everyone's sizes. Record this information below. (Any shop worth its salt will require the groomsmen to be measured by their own trained professionals, but this chart can be used to get preliminary estimates.)

Ringbearer

The boy who accepts this position should dress in a style that coordinates with the men's outfits. He may be dressed in a version of their tuxedos; in his own formal suit; or, if he's very young, in knickers and knee socks, if such a style is in keeping with the rest of the wedding and you can convince him to wear such a thing.

Sizing for Groom's Attendants

	Coat	Sleeve	Neck	Waist	Inseam	Shoe
Best Man						
Groomsmen						
Ushers						
Groom's Father						
Bride's Father						
Ringbearer						

Wedding Attire

* * * * *

Tuxedo Rental Information

	Fitting Date	Pickup Date	Return Date	Cost	Deposit	Balance Due
Best Man						
Formal Wear Shop						
Groomsmen						
Ushers						
Groom's Father						
Bride's Father						
Ringbearer						

Notes

_____
_____
_____
_____
_____

Wedding Attire

The Rings

* * * * *

Banded Together

The Engagement Ring

To be or not to be? The element of surprise, or a cooperative effort? Die-hard romantics look askance at the notion of brides-to-be shopping for their own engagement rings. What happened to the idea of the groom popping the question on bended knee, intriguing little box in hand? Where is the romance in this new world, where the cost of the engagement ring is an item on the budget chart, with spaces to note its estimated cost and who will pay for it?

On the other hand, grooms-to-be are easy targets for diamond-marketing forces, who prey on vulnerable, lovesick adults. "Expect to spend two to three months' salary on the engagement ring," is a common assertion. Meanwhile, the sensible bride might prefer to save that kind of money for a down payment on a house. And assuming she'll wear the ring for all eternity, it would be logical to consult her before rushing out and buying a rock as big as your love (when, in reality, there is no such rock).

In fact, there is a strong case for bringing the bride in on the decision. While the groom may envision the traditional brilliant-cut diamond engagement ring, his intended might prefer an antique emerald. Some women would rather wear one ring on their finger rather than both an engagement ring and a wedding band. A gentleman can keep the cost confidential and still offer his bride some choice in the matter. This is accomplished by meeting with a jeweler, letting him or her know the given price range, and then making an appointment for the two of you to look over the possibilities.

But whether it's the groom's secret or a joint decision, the first thing to do is determine how much can be spent—before the shopping starts. It's also a good idea to familiarize yourself with diamond terminology ("the four Cs") so you'll know how to comparison shop.

The Four Cs

The Gemological Institute of America (GIA) uses a rating system to describe four characteristics of diamonds.

Carat measures a diamond's weight. One carat is equal to 200 milligrams.

Cut refers to the shape of the stone and the number of facets (flat edges). The most popular remains the brilliant cut, but there's also marquis, square, emerald, pear, oval, and heart.

Color is rated on an alphabetical scale ranging from D through Z, with D indicating a rare and expensive jewel, and Z indicating a stone that is yellowish and much less expensive. Most people are happy with the mid-range (K or L, for instance).

Clarity is the diamond's ability to reflect light. The GIA clarity grade runs from FL, which indicates a flawless diamond, to VVS, for very, very small spots, down to I3, which is a diamond that is obviously marred.

* * * * *

Precious Metals

Karat (not to be confused with carat), describes the quantity of pure gold. A 14k ring is 14 parts gold, 10 parts other metals. An 18k ring is 18 parts gold, 6 parts other metals. (24k gold is too soft for wedding rings.) Most wedding rings are a yellowish gold, but if you're looking for a white or silver tone, consider a ring that contains elements of nickel, zinc, copper, palladium, or platinum.

Not all wedding rings are diamonds and gold. Platinum is more precious than gold, and is striking in combination with pearls or colored stones such as rubies or sapphires.

Fun Fact: It takes three tons of ore to produce one ounce of gold, but it takes ten tons of ore to produce one ounce of platinum.

His Wedding Ring, Her Wedding Ring

Most men, as observation will attest, prefer a simple band with no stone. Some choose a two-toned mixture of white and yellow gold or a blend of gold and platinum. The groom usually pays for the bride's wedding ring, and the bride pays for his. Either of you might surprise the other by secretly arranging to have a meaningful message engraved on the inside of the other's ring. You may want your wedding rings to complement one another, but that doesn't necessarily mean buying a matching set. Above all, you should each be delighted with this piece of symbolism that you'll wear on your hand, day in and day out.

Choosing a Reputable Jeweler

Beware of any deal that sounds too good to be true. On the other hand, if you've looked around and you know that you want a marquis-cut diamond that's .50 carats, F color, and VS2 clarity, you can comparison shop at dozens of reputable jewelers. Just be sure that the jeweler can authenticate the quality with a certificate of value, and that the rings can be re-sized if either one of you finds that it doesn't fit quite right.

If you're looking for a piece of original jewelry, many local designers have their own shops. Antique and estate jewelry is available at a growing number of jewelry stores. Once you've purchased the rings, have them insured under your homeowner's or renter's insurance.

Finally, even if you've inherited a ring, you may need to have it re-sized or you may want to update the design and setting. One local couple had the groom's grandparents' rings melted down to create a new set of rings. This takes the symbolism of the wedding ring to a more meaningful level; life and love with no beginning or end, from one generation to the next.

* * * * *

Use the following chart to note ring sizes, preferences, and possible sources as you shop for rings.

Her Ring	His Ring
Her Ring Size	**His Ring Size**
PREFERENCES	PREFERENCES
SOURCE	SOURCE
NOTES	NOTES
Option #1	**Option #1**
SOURCE · COST	SOURCE · COST
NOTES	NOTES
Option #2	**Option #2**
SOURCE · COST	SOURCE · COST
NOTES	NOTES
Option #3	**Option #3**
SOURCE · COST	SOURCE · COST
NOTES	NOTES

The Rings

* * * * *

Profile: ANN & JOHN'S ANTIQUE RINGS

When John Gougebas proposed to Ann Wyckoff, he was pretty sure she would say yes. But he knew that he dared not attempt to choose an engagement ring for her. "She's too picky," says John.

Picky Ann said yes to John, and then started investigating jewelry stores. "I found nothing I liked," she sniffs. "I like white and rose gold, and most stores have only new gold. Not wanting to custom-order a ring, or pay the 300-percent mark-up most stores charge, I decided to look for an antique ring."

Ann feels that antique rings have more detail and character than new ones. Not only that, good-quality gems were much less expensive in antique shops than in jewelry stores. She also learned that estate jewelry typically describes jewelry from the 1950s or later, while antique jewelry is older. Before visiting an antique store, Ann would call ahead to make sure they had more than a couple rings. Another option, and the one which ultimately worked for Ann and John, are traveling antique shows. Here, couples are able to visit five to ten booths selling antique jewelry from all over the country. To ensure a fair price, the more expensive rings have official appraisal papers. The less expensive rings (under $1000) can be appraised on-site at a competing booth.

Ann found her engagement ring at just such an antique show. The ring is platinum with a ruby and eight diamonds, and dates from 1900 to 1920. She found her wedding band just weeks before the wedding at another show; it's a white gold band with tiny diamonds. John's wedding band was purchased from an antique store. It's made of rose gold and has a grape leaf pattern in it. Ann and John are happy with their choices, even though her wedding and engagement rings don't "match," nor does her band match his. The pair personalized their antique rings by having them engraved with their initials and wedding date.

NOTES

_____

_____

_____

_____

_____

_____

_____

_____

_____

The Rings

Notes

SERVICES

TRANSPORTATION

✻

FLOWERS

✻

MUSIC

✻

PHOTOGRAPHY & VIDEOGRAPHY

SERVICES

Transportation

✲ ✲ ✲ ✲ ✲

Getting Around

Transportation for Out-of-Town Guests

Before contemplating the more interesting topic of your own conveyance, be a good host and consider the needs of your out-of-town guests. It may be as simple as asking a friend or relative to share a ride. Elderly relatives or guests with disabilities need special consideration. If you're inviting families with young children, ask if they'll need to rent or borrow car seats.

Guests who will need help with transportation:

Name
Special Considerations
_____
_____

Name
Special Considerations
_____
_____

Name
Special Considerations
_____
_____

Name
Special Considerations
_____
_____

Name
Special Considerations
_____
_____

Name
Special Considerations
_____
_____

Name
Special Considerations
_____
_____

Parking

Will there be enough parking space at the ceremony and reception sites? If not, you might have to employ some kind of shuttle service for guests. Is there any construction planned that might create parking or accessibility problems? If the ceremony and reception will be at a private residence, check with the local police about parking ordinances. Depending on the location, consider hiring a valet parking service for guests.

Special arrangements for parking at the ceremony and/or reception site:

_____
_____

Making a Grand Entrance (and Exit)

Teresa Paulson arrived at her courthouse ceremony in a horse-drawn carriage, accompanied by her parents. After the wedding, she and her new husband, Tim Cook, rode off together into the sunset in the same carriage. Old-fashioned conveyances are especially romantic, but a couple's arrival and departure can be dramatic whether the mode of transportation is classic, modern, or a mixture of the two. The entire wedding party might arrive in matching limos, and at the end of the wedding the couple could take off in a hot-air balloon. In wintry locales, the bride might pull up to the church in a horse-drawn sleigh, which could then take guests for rides during the reception. In summer, the couple might depart on a pair of matching Harleys, wave goodbye from a classic convertible, or set sail in a boat if the wedding takes place on the waterfront.

The possibilities are limitless. There are plenty of reputable transportation companies available, including livery services offering limousines and classic cars. When choosing a company, make sure that they're fully licensed and insured; meet face-to-face with a representative of the company, and ask to see the exact cars that will be used (get the vehicle identification number [VIN] committed in the contract). Rates are by the hour, usually with a minimum of two or three hours. Ask about overtime rates (just in case), deposit requirements, tipping policies, amenities, and what the drivers will wear.

Consider hiring enough cars to transport the entire wedding party. That way, parents and grandparents can be taken immediately to the reception site (just behind the newlyweds), arriving in advance of the guests to take their places in the receiving line.

Choosing a Transportation Company

Company #1

CONTACT _____ PHONE _____

TYPE OF CONVEYANCE _____

RATE INFO _____ MINIMUM _____ OVERTIME _____

AMOUNT OF DEPOSIT DUE _____ DATE DUE _____

Company #2

CONTACT _____ PHONE _____

TYPE OF CONVEYANCE _____

RATE INFO _____ MINIMUM _____ OVERTIME _____

AMOUNT OF DEPOSIT DUE _____ DATE DUE _____

* * * * *

Company #3

Contact Phone

Type of Conveyance

___

Rate Info Minimum Overtime

Amount of Deposit Due Date Due

Once you choose a transportation company, you'll want to sign a contract that includes the date, time, and place of pickup(s); the number of people to be transported, the number of vehicles and their VINs; hourly rate and the number of hours; any additional fees; deposit required and due date of deposit; the service's cancellation policy, and liability in case of accident, injury, or damage to the vehicle.

Before the big day, drivers should receive a schedule of wedding-day events, directions and addresses, and a list of the order in which you and the wedding party will arrive at the ceremony, leave for the reception, and depart the reception.

Use the following charts to ensure that all wedding-day transportation is arranged. Before the day of the wedding, appoint one individual who will have this information at his or her fingertips. That way, if Aunt Martha is nowhere to be found, someone can call the driver and find out what's going on.

To The Ceremony

Transport Company

Phone Number(s)

Contact Name

Pickup (When & Where)

Who will be transported

___

Transportation

67

* * * * *

To The Reception

Transport Company
_____

Phone Number(s)
_____

Contact Name
_____

Pickup (When & Where)
_____
_____

Who will be transported
_____
_____
_____
_____
_____
_____
_____
_____
_____
_____
_____
_____
_____

From the Reception to Home

Transport Company
_____

Phone Number(s)
_____

Contact Name
_____

Pickup (When & Where)
_____
_____

Who will be transported
_____
_____
_____
_____
_____
_____
_____
_____
_____
_____
_____
_____
_____

Transportation

Notes

Flowers

* * * * *

First Considerations

If money were no object, most brides would go crazy with flowers—what could be nicer than artful arrangements of freshly cut blossoms at every turn? But even if your budget is limited, your wedding day can be abloom in flowers. One easy way to accomplish this would be to choose an indoor or outdoor garden as your wedding site.

If the question of flowers is not so easy to handle, take stock of your wedding site, ideally at the time of day the ceremony will be held. Notice the amount of sunlight coming through the windows, the way the sun affects stained glass, and the colors in the room. The light and color of the room will influence the flowers that you choose. Are there fire restrictions regarding the use of candles, or liturgical seasons that may dictate the use of certain kinds of flowers?

For centuries, bridal bouquets have been as white as the traditional wedding dress. Now most brides incorporate their favorite colors into their bouquets. To add that personal touch, florists are using hydrangeas and herbs from the bride's own garden, or incorporating blooms from the family's prized rose bush. When it comes to flowers at the wedding, find your inspiration from the world around you. Find your florist by asking around.

Finding a Florist

When you're out and about in the months before the wedding, notice floral arrangements. Ask for referrals from friends, or from the manager of your reception site. Start shopping for a florist in earnest several months before the wedding. Remember, there are florists and there are floral designers. If your wedding site has some aesthetic challenges—a civic atmosphere or lighting problems—you'll want to call upon someone who calls himself or herself a designer.

You'll want to talk to several florists or designers in order to find one whose style matches your own. Reception and ceremony site arrangements often incorporate candles, balloons, trellises, and archways. A florist may be able to supply an aisle runner, kneeling benches, or other wedding "hardware."

Florist/Designer #1

Contact _____ Phone _____

Floral Plan _____

_____

_____

Ideas for Wedding Site _____

_____

_____

Flowers

* * * * *

Florist/Designer #2

CONTACT   PHONE

FLORAL PLAN

IDEAS FOR WEDDING SITE

Florist/Designer #3

CONTACT   PHONE

FLORAL PLAN

IDEAS FOR WEDDING SITE

Your contract with the florist should stipulate the delivery time and date, the total price, and the cancellation policy. Can the florist guarantee that the flowers you specified will be available and fresh? If there's a question about availability, is there an acceptable substitution? You may be required to put down a deposit, but don't pay the whole bill until the flowers have been delivered.

If you'll need to enlist the help of a friend or family member to transfer floral arrangements from the ceremony to the reception site, note such arrangements here:

TRANSFER PERSON

KNOWS WHAT'S EXPECTED

TIME OF TRANSFER

You may also want to arrange to have someone take the floral arrangements home after the reception, or offer them to departing guests.

Flowers

* * * * *

For the Wedding Party

The Bridal Bouquet

There are several styles of bridal bouquets. A cascading bouquet can have a dramatic effect, especially when carried by a tall bride. A smaller woman or a bride wearing an ornate dress might prefer to carry a nosegay. A crescent or arm arrangement nestles along the bride's arm. In lieu of a bouquet, some brides carry a few miniature sunflowers or a spray of calla lilies, or the family Bible with one or two white roses. Your florist may suggest a separate "throwing bouquet" so that you can preserve the one that you carry down the aisle. Some bridal bouquets have a detachable corsage for the bride to wear as she leaves on her honeymoon.

Flower Girl

She may sprinkle petals on the bridal path, or distribute roses to guests from her basket.

Bride's Attendants

The maid/matron of honor/best woman might have a bouquet that's different in color or slightly larger than the other attendants' arrangements.

Corsages & Boutonnieres

The grandmothers' and mothers' corsages should be chosen with their dresses in mind. Boutonnieres for the groom's attendants, the ringbearer, ushers, fathers, and grandfathers will likely consist of a single blossom. They should all be the same, while the groom's boutonniere might be a little different or more elaborate.

For the Ceremony

First, give consideration to any rules regarding floral arrangements in a church or synagogue. Obviously, you'll need to consider the site's size and the lighting. The floral arrangements should direct everyone's attention to the altar, with arrangements that are large enough to be seen from the back of the room. In a Jewish ceremony, the vows are spoken under a *chuppah*, which is covered with greens and flowers. In an outdoor ceremony, vows may be exchanged under an archway decorated with blooms and greenery.

The aisle may be decorated with flowers and ribbons, wreaths, and topiaries. Wreaths can be used as centerpieces during the reception; simply lay them flat on the table and place candles in the center. Topiaries can also serve double-duty, as long as the florist designs them so that they aren't so tall and wide as to stop conversation across the dinner table. Potted plants can be used at both the ceremony and reception, and later be planted in the couple's own flower garden, creating heirloom blooms.

For the Reception

Table decorations and centerpieces should complement table linens. Such centerpieces may be flowering plants or cut flowers in baskets. Larger potted plants or small trees can be draped with twinkle lights, and used to jazz up an entryway or to draw attention to the head table. (Small trees and topiaries can sometimes be rented from the florist.) You may want the florist to decorate the cake table or provide flowers with which to decorate the cake.

* * * * *

The Floral Plan

Wedding Party & Family	Description	Cost	Deliver to	Time
Bride				
Bouquet				
Flowers for Hair				
Going-away Corsage				
Bride's Attendants				
Maid of Honor				
Bridesmaids				
QTY:				
Flower Girl				
Flowers for Hair				
Groom				
Boutonniere				
Groom's Attendants				
Best Man				
Groomsmen				
QTY:				
Ushers				
QTY:				
Ringbearer				
Corsage/Boutonniere				
Bride's Mother				
Groom's Mother				
Bride's Father				
Groom's Father				
Grandmothers				
QTY:				
Grandfathers				
QTY:				
Other				
(aunts, step-parents, wedding helpers)				
Corsages				
QTY:				
Boutonnieres				
QTY:				

Flowers

* * * * *

The Floral Plan (cont.)

	Description	Cost	Deliver to	Time
Ceremony				
Number of Arrangements				
Altar				
Aisle				
Other				
Other				
Other				
Reception				
Wedding Party's Table				
Qty:				
Guests' Tables				
Qty:				
Cake & Knife				
Guest Book Table				
Other				
Other Arrangements				

Florist (final selection) _____ Contact _____ Phone _____

Total Cost _____ Amount of Deposit _____ Date Due _____

Equipment/Plants Rented from Florist _____

To Be Returned By (Person) _____ Date/Time of Return _____ Cost of Rentals _____

Flowers

Notes

* * * * *

Music

* * * * *

The Ceremony

As your guests begin to arrive, a lilting melody beckons them to the site of the impending nuptials. The notes play on seamlessly while guests are ushered to their places. Finally, the mother of the bride is seated. The groom stands at the altar. The royal blare of a trumpet announces the bride's arrival from the wings.

Music at the ceremony sets the mood: The feeling that something grand and dramatic is about to happen. The mood may be light and lyrical or smooth and sophisticated. Your choice of music not only sets the tone, it may be an intentional or unintentional window to your soul. Like Freud's slip, perhaps it shouldn't be showing. A case in point:

At a wedding in the 1970s, as guests took their seats and waited for the processional to begin, the church organist played the notes of a familiar tune. It was a popular song, the theme from M*A*S*H. The unsung lyrics of the song played in the head of at least one guest. Suddenly, one 13 year old among them was stricken by uncontrollable laughter. "Do you know what the words to this song are?" she asked her father, who was attempting unsuccessfully to shush the child. "It's 'Suicide is Painless,'" she explained. "At a wedding!" The father started laughing, too, and the epidemic spread.

The lesson is this: Make sure that the message sent by the music is one you wish to communicate. Perhaps the bride and groom were familiar with the lyrics to the M*A*S*H theme song, but in retrospect, this seems unlikely.

Another consideration is that many churches do not allow secular music. That means that the traditional "Bridal Chorus" (a.k.a. "Here Comes the Bride") and "Wedding March" cannot be played in some houses of worship.

Once you know the rules in your house of worship, you'll know your options. In a church, you may call on the services of the music director, the choir, or the church organist. You may wish to hire a harpist, a guitar soloist, a vocalist, a trumpeter, or a string quartet. A musically talented friend or relative may be happy to sing a song or play the piano during your ceremony. Barring that, you can hire musicians through local music schools and entertainment agencies.

Musicians who are experienced with wedding gigs can offer ideas about what pieces they might play. There are four phases in a wedding ceremony, musically speaking: The *prelude* is the 20 to 30 minute period during which guests are seated (not a time that you want your guests to be humming, "suicide is painless"). Then there's the *processional*, the here-comes-the-bride part, which leads to the ceremony itself. During the ceremony, you may want to play two or three songs or hymns that are especially meaningful to the two of you. The *recessional* music should be jubilant—now your lives have begun! A few years ago, friends of mine chose the Beatle's tune "When I'm Sixty-Four" as music for the recessional. The lyrics were printed in the guest programs so that we could all sing along: "Will you still need me, will you still feed me, when I'm sixty-four?"

Whatever music you choose, be familiar with the beat. The bride should practice walking down the aisle to the processional music, and the two of you might want to practice the recessional together.

Music Sources

When choosing musicians who will perform at your wedding, the cardinal rule is this: Make sure you've heard them play before you sign them up.

Agencies will charge a fee for helping you find the right entertainment, but the advantage is that you'll know you're working with professionals who have experience working weddings gigs.

Profile: **RUSS AND LORI'S LYRICAL WEDDING**

As part of premarital counseling at Lori Entinger's hometown church, Russ Rogers was asked to write a poem for his bride-to-be. The groom did the required homework, and then earned some extra credit. Russ's profession in life is entertainment, as half of a musical team called "Kit and Kaboodle." So naturally—and unknown to Lori until the ceremony—Russ set his poem to music. Andy LaCasse, a.k.a. "Kit" and Russ's best man, sang the song on behalf of the groom. Entitled "I Can See the Angel (Hiding Inside of You)," it was a wonderful surprise to the bride. The thought-balloons of many female guests were nearly visible above their heads as they glanced at their own partners, thinking, "Hmph, I bet he'd never write a song like that for me."

After the ceremony, Lori was heard to say, "I think I married a really good guy." The song's lyrics were an unabashed declaration of love, and why not? There's no better time than a wedding to let your lover know—along with everyone else—exactly how you feel.

NOTES

_____
_____
_____
_____
_____

* * * * *

Use the space below to record information about musicians for the ceremony.

Musician #1   INSTRUMENT

MUSICAL PIECE(S) TO BE PERFORMED

Musician #2   INSTRUMENT

MUSICAL PIECE(S) TO BE PERFORMED

Musician #3   INSTRUMENT

MUSICAL PIECE(S) TO BE PERFORMED

Musician #4   INSTRUMENT

MUSICAL PIECE(S) TO BE PERFORMED

Music

List the musical pieces that will be performed during the ceremony, from prelude through recessional.

CEREMONIAL MUSIC

PRELUDE

_____

_____

_____

PROCESSIONAL

_____

_____

CEREMONY

_____

_____

_____

_____

_____

_____

RECESSIONAL

_____

_____

_____

_____

THE RECEPTION

Music at the reception may begin as background instrumentals while guests file through the reception line and mingle during the cocktail hour. Later the music moves to the foreground—whether it's classical, jazz, ethnic, or techno-funk. It may take the form of a dance band, an orchestra, a jazz ensemble, or a compilation of your own pre-recorded favorites. If you do opt for live musicians, make certain that you have heard their stuff, and that the volume of their sound system is compatible with the reception site. You don't want your guests to be blasted out of the room.

According to musician and writer Jeff Mueller, there are four things you want out of a reception band: versatility, adaptability, musical skill, and professionalism. Versatility means the band can perform a wide range of musical styles, thus making sure that guests of all ages are moved to stomp their feet, if not actually dance. Adaptability means the band can read the crowd and sense what's working, what's not working, and then adjust their performance accordingly. Musical skill can only be gauged by listening to the band. Professionalism is the question of how they conduct themselves: How much experience do they have performing at wedding receptions? Do they have a standard contract? How will the group dress for the wedding?

Generally, D.J.s should meet the same criteria. Some D.J.s perform dramatic light shows or create a disco atmosphere.

* * * * *

Some are more reserved, while others interact with the guests, tell jokes and introduce your Uncle Morty's samba act. Whatever their style, make sure it's right for your wedding.

    The bandleader or the D.J. may act as a sort of master of ceremonies. An experienced entertainer will have a playlist from which you can pick the songs you love and nix the ones you don't want. Ask the bandleader whether the musicians that you've seen perform will be the very ones showing up at the reception. Also, find out if the band plays pre-recorded music while they're on break (and how often do they take a break?). Whether you employ a D.J. or a band, before booking the act make sure that the entertainers' equipment is compatible with the site's electrical system.

Use the space below to record information about entertainment for the reception.

Musicians/D.J. # 1 (CIRCLE ONE)

CONTACT   PHONE

NOTES ON STYLE

FREQUENCY & LENGTH OF BREAKS

RECORDED MUSIC TO
COVER BREAKS? ☐ YES ☐ NO
RATE (PER HOUR)   OVERTIME RATE   TOTAL

Musicians/D.J. # 2 (CIRCLE ONE)

CONTACT   PHONE

NOTES ON STYLE

FREQUENCY & LENGTH OF BREAKS

RECORDED MUSIC TO
COVER BREAKS? ☐ YES ☐ NO
RATE (PER HOUR)   OVERTIME RATE   TOTAL

Musicians/D.J. # 3 (CIRCLE ONE)

CONTACT   PHONE

NOTES ON STYLE

FREQUENCY & LENGTH OF BREAKS

RECORDED MUSIC TO
COVER BREAKS? ☐ YES ☐ NO
RATE (PER HOUR)   OVERTIME RATE   TOTAL

When you choose a band or D.J., circle the corresponding information above. Your contract with them should specify the time they're expected to show up, as well as all charges, required deposits, and cancellation policies.

Notes

✶ ✶ ✶ ✶

Photography & Videography

✶ ✶ ✶ ✶ ✶

Picture This

When it comes to capturing the memories of your wedding, it's best to leave the work to the professionals. Of course, if friends and family members want to take pictures, that will only increase the chances of a great variety of photographs. You may even want to provide disposable cameras at each guest table. (Be sure to designate a person to collect them at the end of the reception.) Professional photographers offer varied services at varied prices. It's best to start shopping for these services as soon as you set the wedding date, since popular photographers may be booked up to a year in advance.

Choosing a Photographer

You're looking for a photographer with whom you feel a rapport and compatibility, not only in terms of his or her personality, but in terms of style. As a couple, you and your fiancé will be sharing the most important day of your life with this person, and he or she will be responsible for capturing the memories created at your wedding.

A wedding photographer's approach may be that of a classic portraitist, that of a photojournalist, or something in-between. Still, most photographers have a sensibility that's predominantly one or the other.

Portrait photography is the most traditional approach by wedding photographers, but this style need not produce unimaginative photographs. The modern portrait photographer uses outdoor locations as well as special filters, lighting, and development processes to capture the spirit of the two of you as a couple, or to create a memorable fantasy. At the other end of the spectrum is the wedding photographer who uses a photojournalistic approach to record the event. Like the portrait photographer, he or she will take the requisite photos of the bridal party and important family members, but the photojournalist's eye is on the moments that are not posed. Most wedding photographers do not fall strictly into one category or the other, but it's important to understand these two distinct styles.

As a preliminary step, compile a list of 6 to 12 potential photographers. Consult friends who were recently married in your area, the manager of your reception site, and bridal shows for references. In the space on page 84, jot down names and phone numbers. Call each one and ask if they'll send you a brochure and a price list, or arrange a time to meet them and view their work.

From your list, narrow the field to two or three candidates to seriously interview. Set up appointments with these photographers and be prepared to ask and answer questions. (Large studios often employ several photographers. Make sure the person you interview is the person who will be working for you.)

As you speak with each photographer,

* * * * *

leaf through his or her portfolio. Do you like the pictures? Are they of good quality? Do they capture the individuality of the ceremony? Ask the photographer if he or she is familiar with your wedding site. (And if not, would he or she become familiar with it before the wedding?) Many photographers take a mixture of color film and black and white film, others shoot exclusively in one or the other.

Black and white photography creates a timeless image and has recently made a comeback. Black and white prints may be hand-tinted, sepia-toned, or shot using "infrared" film—a special process that creates a dramatic effect. If the photographer is experienced in these techniques, look at samples of his or her work.

The photographer can help you compile a list of photographs that he or she will take. (If you'll be married in a church or synagogue, check into possible restrictions on cameras during the ceremony.) Traditionally, a bridal portrait is taken for newspaper wedding announcements, but many couples now choose to have a formal wedding portrait taken before the wedding. (For the purposes of a newspaper announcement, send an 8x10 black and white picture to the paper's society editor at least one week before the wedding.) The bridal or wedding portrait can be taken after the bride's final fitting. She may consider it a dress rehearsal for the wedding, a chance to make sure she's got the perfect hairstyle, make-up and jewelry. (No need to go overboard on the make-up for the sake of the camera—this isn't television!)

Photographers may charge a basic rate for a certain number of hours on the day of the wedding, with albums for the couple and for their parents offered as part of a package plan at an additional cost. Ask about rates and the cost of extra prints. Also ask how long negatives are kept on file (three to five years should be the average). Check the level of professionalism by asking how much experience the photographer has had shooting weddings. Many work with an assistant whose job it is to make sure that everyone—particularly the bride—looks their best.

Most importantly, go into this interview with a clear idea of what each of you expects as bride and groom. The bride may want a dozen portraits taken with various sets of family members, while the groom may not want to spend half his wedding day posing for pictures. Settle this between yourselves before you meet with photographers. (One simple solution is to have most of the portraits taken before the ceremony.) You want to make sure that your photographer is capable of producing the pictures you want, so you'll have to be able to identify and communicate your expectations.

Photography & Videography

* * * * *

Narrowing the Field

Photographer # 1

Contact   Phone

Address   Appointment Time & Date

Notes on Style

Favorite Shots from Portfolio

Notes on Size of Prints, Style of Album(s)

# of Hours   Base Rate   Overtime Rate

Cost of Wedding Album

Cost of Parents' Album

Cost of Extra Prints   8x10   5x7   Other

Total Estimated Cost

Photographer # 2

Contact   Phone

Address   Appointment Time & Date

Notes on Style

Favorite Shots from Portfolio

Notes on Size of Prints, Style of Album(s)

# of Hours   Base Rate   Overtime Rate

Cost of Wedding Album

Cost of Parents' Album

Cost of Extra Prints   8x10   5x7   Other

Total Estimated Cost

Photography & Videography

* * * * *

Photographer # 3

CONTACT   PHONE

ADDRESS   APPOINTMENT TIME & DATE

NOTES ON STYLE

FAVORITE SHOTS FROM PORTFOLIO

NOTES ON SIZE OF PRINTS, STYLE OF ALBUM(S)

OF HOURS   BASE RATE   OVERTIME RATE

COST OF WEDDING ALBUM

COST OF PARENTS' ALBUM

COST OF EXTRA PRINTS 8x10   5x7   OTHER

TOTAL ESTIMATED COST

When you make a final decision regarding the photographer, record specific information below.

Photographer

CONTACT   PHONE

ADDRESS

WEDDING PORTRAIT   TIME & DATE

TIME & PLACE OF ARRIVAL ON WEDDING DATE

GONE OVER LIST OF
REQUIRED PHOTOS? ☐ YES ☐ NO

DATE PROOFS READY

DATE ALBUMS & PRINTS AVAILABLE

FINAL ESTIMATE

VIDEOGRAPHY

Although many couples choose to have their weddings videotaped, there are others who would rather remember their wedding as a romantic comedy that plays only in their heads. The latter is a legitimate decision, no matter what the videobug in your family has to say about it.

    That said, if you do want a videotape of the big day, you might at least bypass the aforementioned amateur videobug. Wouldn't you rather this person be present as a participating guest, rather than as a camera-wielding obstruction? (You can

Photography & Videography

* * * * *

probably think of a more tactful way to say this, and it is possible to politely decline such offers.) On the other hand, if you're convinced that the amateur videographer will do a good job, by all means go for it. Just be sure he or she uses high-quality videotape. You may also want to check area film schools and colleges for film students who moonlight as wedding videographers.

Whether you go with an amateur or a pro, the first thing to do is check the restrictions in the church or synagogue regarding videotaping the ceremony. The wedding and reception sites may pose lighting challenges, which should be addressed by the videographer in advance of the wedding day.

Choosing a Videographer

Some photography studios offer videography, too. There are also companies who do only videography. Either way, it's best to work with a pair of videographers using two cameras—this is to make sure that the best possible footage is captured from just the right angle, as well as to provide a backup in case of equipment failure. Depending on the video editor's level of expertise and individual style, the wedding video may be jazzed up with graphics, voice-overs, a montage of still photographs, and other techniques. You want a videographer who will blend into the crowd, one who will be sensitive to the individual guest's level of comfort with the camera.

Before interviewing videographers, compile a list of candidates. Ask for sample videos along with their price lists.

Videographer # 1

CONTACT _____ PHONE _____

ADDRESS _____ APPOINTMENT TIME & DATE _____

NOTES ON STYLE
_____
_____
_____

NOTES ON EDITING
_____
_____
_____

FINISHED LENGTH OF VIDEO
_____

OF HOURS _____ FEE FOR EXTRA COPIES _____

TOTAL ESTIMATED COST _____

Videographer # 2

CONTACT _____ PHONE _____

ADDRESS _____ APPOINTMENT TIME & DATE _____

NOTES ON STYLE
_____
_____
_____

NOTES ON EDITING
_____

Photography & Videography

✶ ✶ ✶ ✶ ✶

FINISHED LENGTH OF VIDEO

\# OF HOURS   FEE FOR EXTRA COPIES

TOTAL ESTIMATED COST

Videographer # 3

CONTACT   PHONE

ADDRESS   APPOINTMENT TIME & DATE

NOTES ON STYLE

NOTES ON EDITING

FINISHED LENGTH OF VIDEO

\# OF HOURS   FEE FOR EXTRA COPIES

TOTAL ESTIMATED COST

When you make a final decision regarding the videographer, record specific information below.

Videographer

CONTACT   PHONE

ADDRESS   APPOINTMENT TIME & DATE

SIZE OF FILM CREW   NUMBER OF CAMERAS

TIME & PLACE OF ARRIVAL ON WEDDING DATE

PRELIMINARY VIEWING
BEFORE EDITING? ☐ YES ☐ NO

IF SO, DATE?

DATE OF DELIVERY OF FINISHED TAPE

FINAL ESTIMATE

Photography & Videography

Notes

✶✶✶✶✶

Gifts, Parties & Honeymoon

GIVING & RECEIVING GIFTS

✴

PARTIES

✴

YOUR HONEYMOON

GIFTS, PARTIES
& HONEYMOON

Giving & Receiving Gifts

✶ ✶ ✶ ✶ ✶

Giving

As the wedding approaches and preparations become more frenzied, don't lose sight of the friends and family who are helping you make it happen. Whether it's a best friend who has accompanied you to countless fittings, or a future mother-in-law who takes a firm stand against dispensing advice, it's likely you've been touched by the support, guidance, and just plain hard work offered by those around you.

It's standard practice to present the attendants with gifts at the rehearsal dinner, but there will be others who deserve some token of appreciation. There's no need to bust your budget with gratitude, as long as the gift is something that will stand the test of time and has personal meaning to the recipient. The bridesmaids might receive a special treasure box for their dressers, birthstone jewelry, or a silver picture frame. The groomsmen might be given a fountain pen or a silver cocktail jigger. For the flower girl and the ringbearer, consider a fancy kaleidoscope—kids are fascinated with them. Your parents might enjoy a formal wedding portrait in a frame—or perhaps tickets to a play. Take stock of any other people who have contributed in a meaningful way to your wedding—the officiant who helped you work through some premarital jitters, the cousin who's throwing you a shower, or the co-worker who's covering for you while you're on your honeymoon.

Bride and groom may wish to exchange gifts as well. Engraved jewelry or framed portraits are a traditional choice. Others give luggage or a videocamera to take on the honeymoon.

Notes on Gift Ideas

_____

_____

_____

_____

_____

_____

_____

_____

_____

_____

_____

_____

* * * * *

Gifts for Attendants

	Gift Description	Cost
Best Woman		
Brides's Attendants		
Best Man		
Groom's Attendants		
Ushers		
Parents		
Other		

Giving & Receiving Gifts

* * * * *

RECEIVING

Gift Registry

Thanks to computers and hand-held scanners, the modern bride and groom can walk through a department store and register for everything from washcloths to Waterford crystal. Whether you're younger or older, on your first marriage or a remarriage, you'll probably want to register for gifts at two or three stores. If you're starting out with a total lack of household items, then it's best that you make conscious choices now about such things as china patterns, saucepan preferences, and bed and bath decor. That way, your marital home will closely resemble the home of your dreams. Even if you've both been living on your own for years, a gift registry enables you to take stock of what you will bring to your new home, what ought to be replaced, and what items will be lacking.

When gift registry is mentioned, most people think of major department stores. But gift registry is available at all kinds of stores, including national chains like Target, Crate & Barrel and HomePlace, as well as small specialty shops, hardware stores, and camping supply outlets. See the Resources section for a comprehensive Bridal Registry listing. Once you've registered at a couple of places, write down their names and phone numbers and give copies to both sets of parents. Keep the names by your own phone, and give out this information, guilt-free, when asked. Remember, you're doing people a favor.

Thank-Yous

Gifts may arrive before, during, or well after the wedding, and you should try to respond with a thank-you note within two weeks of each gift's receipt. Now that we've dealt with the greed (just kidding, just kidding), let's move on to gratitude. You may have ordered personalized thank-you notes along with your invitations and announcements, or you may have purchased plain notecards from your local card shop. Either is fine; the important thing is that you graciously thank each gift-giver.

If you're sharing the task of writing thank-you notes—which is only fair, since the gift is intended for the two of you—extra care will have to be taken to ensure that no gift-giver goes unthanked. Try to keep up with the process as the gifts are received. You can keep track of gifts received and thank-you notes sent in the following pages.

Space for 160 thank-yous is provided on the following pages.

Giving & Receiving Gifts

* * * * *

NAME	NAME
GIFT DESCRIPTION	GIFT DESCRIPTION
THANK-YOU WRITTEN BY	THANK-YOU WRITTEN BY
DATE SENT ☐	DATE SENT ☐
NAME	NAME
GIFT DESCRIPTION	GIFT DESCRIPTION
THANK-YOU WRITTEN BY	THANK-YOU WRITTEN BY
DATE SENT ☐	DATE SENT ☐
NAME	NAME
GIFT DESCRIPTION	GIFT DESCRIPTION
THANK-YOU WRITTEN BY	THANK-YOU WRITTEN BY
DATE SENT ☐	DATE SENT ☐
NAME	NAME
GIFT DESCRIPTION	GIFT DESCRIPTION
THANK-YOU WRITTEN BY	THANK-YOU WRITTEN BY
DATE SENT ☐	DATE SENT ☐
NAME	NAME
GIFT DESCRIPTION	GIFT DESCRIPTION
THANK-YOU WRITTEN BY	THANK-YOU WRITTEN BY
DATE SENT ☐	DATE SENT ☐
NAME	NAME
GIFT DESCRIPTION	GIFT DESCRIPTION
THANK-YOU WRITTEN BY	THANK-YOU WRITTEN BY
DATE SENT ☐	DATE SENT ☐
NAME	NAME
GIFT DESCRIPTION	GIFT DESCRIPTION
THANK-YOU WRITTEN BY	THANK-YOU WRITTEN BY
DATE SENT ☐	DATE SENT ☐

Giving & Receiving Gifts

✶ ✶ ✶ ✶ ✶

NAME
GIFT DESCRIPTION

THANK-YOU WRITTEN BY
DATE SENT ☐

NAME
GIFT DESCRIPTION

THANK-YOU WRITTEN BY
DATE SENT ☐

NAME
GIFT DESCRIPTION

THANK-YOU WRITTEN BY
DATE SENT ☐

NAME
GIFT DESCRIPTION

THANK-YOU WRITTEN BY
DATE SENT ☐

NAME
GIFT DESCRIPTION

THANK-YOU WRITTEN BY
DATE SENT ☐

NAME
GIFT DESCRIPTION

THANK-YOU WRITTEN BY
DATE SENT ☐

NAME
GIFT DESCRIPTION

THANK-YOU WRITTEN BY
DATE SENT ☐

NAME
GIFT DESCRIPTION

THANK-YOU WRITTEN BY
DATE SENT ☐

NAME
GIFT DESCRIPTION

THANK-YOU WRITTEN BY
DATE SENT ☐

NAME
GIFT DESCRIPTION

THANK-YOU WRITTEN BY
DATE SENT ☐

NAME
GIFT DESCRIPTION

THANK-YOU WRITTEN BY
DATE SENT ☐

NAME
GIFT DESCRIPTION

THANK-YOU WRITTEN BY
DATE SENT ☐

NAME
GIFT DESCRIPTION

THANK-YOU WRITTEN BY
DATE SENT ☐

NAME
GIFT DESCRIPTION

THANK-YOU WRITTEN BY
DATE SENT ☐

Giving & Receiving Gifts

* * * * *

Name	Name
Gift Description	Gift Description

Thank-you written by   Thank-you written by
                              Date Sent ☐   Date Sent ☐

Name	Name
Gift Description	Gift Description

Thank-you written by   Thank-you written by
                              Date Sent ☐   Date Sent ☐

Name	Name
Gift Description	Gift Description

Thank-you written by   Thank-you written by
                              Date Sent ☐   Date Sent ☐

Name	Name
Gift Description	Gift Description

Thank-you written by   Thank-you written by
                              Date Sent ☐   Date Sent ☐

Name	Name
Gift Description	Gift Description

Thank-you written by   Thank-you written by
                              Date Sent ☐   Date Sent ☐

Name	Name
Gift Description	Gift Description

Thank-you written by   Thank-you written by
                              Date Sent ☐   Date Sent ☐

Name	Name
Gift Description	Gift Description

Thank-you written by   Thank-you written by
                              Date Sent ☐   Date Sent ☐

Giving & Receiving Gifts

* * * * *

NAME _____
GIFT DESCRIPTION _____

THANK-YOU WRITTEN BY _____
_____ DATE SENT ☐

NAME _____
GIFT DESCRIPTION _____

THANK-YOU WRITTEN BY _____
_____ DATE SENT ☐

NAME _____
GIFT DESCRIPTION _____

THANK-YOU WRITTEN BY _____
_____ DATE SENT ☐

NAME _____
GIFT DESCRIPTION _____

THANK-YOU WRITTEN BY _____
_____ DATE SENT ☐

NAME _____
GIFT DESCRIPTION _____

THANK-YOU WRITTEN BY _____
_____ DATE SENT ☐

NAME _____
GIFT DESCRIPTION _____

THANK-YOU WRITTEN BY _____
_____ DATE SENT ☐

NAME _____
GIFT DESCRIPTION _____

THANK-YOU WRITTEN BY _____
_____ DATE SENT ☐

NAME _____
GIFT DESCRIPTION _____

THANK-YOU WRITTEN BY _____
_____ DATE SENT ☐

NAME _____
GIFT DESCRIPTION _____

THANK-YOU WRITTEN BY _____
_____ DATE SENT ☐

NAME _____
GIFT DESCRIPTION _____

THANK-YOU WRITTEN BY _____
_____ DATE SENT ☐

NAME _____
GIFT DESCRIPTION _____

THANK-YOU WRITTEN BY _____
_____ DATE SENT ☐

NAME _____
GIFT DESCRIPTION _____

THANK-YOU WRITTEN BY _____
_____ DATE SENT ☐

NAME _____
GIFT DESCRIPTION _____

THANK-YOU WRITTEN BY _____
_____ DATE SENT ☐

NAME _____
GIFT DESCRIPTION _____

THANK-YOU WRITTEN BY _____
_____ DATE SENT ☐

Giving & Receiving Gifts

* * * * *

NAME _____
GIFT DESCRIPTION _____

THANK-YOU WRITTEN BY _____
_____ DATE SENT ☐

NAME _____
GIFT DESCRIPTION _____

THANK-YOU WRITTEN BY _____
_____ DATE SENT ☐

NAME _____
GIFT DESCRIPTION _____

THANK-YOU WRITTEN BY _____
_____ DATE SENT ☐

NAME _____
GIFT DESCRIPTION _____

THANK-YOU WRITTEN BY _____
_____ DATE SENT ☐

NAME _____
GIFT DESCRIPTION _____

THANK-YOU WRITTEN BY _____
_____ DATE SENT ☐

NAME _____
GIFT DESCRIPTION _____

THANK-YOU WRITTEN BY _____
_____ DATE SENT ☐

NAME _____
GIFT DESCRIPTION _____

THANK-YOU WRITTEN BY _____
_____ DATE SENT ☐

NAME _____
GIFT DESCRIPTION _____

THANK-YOU WRITTEN BY _____
_____ DATE SENT ☐

NAME _____
GIFT DESCRIPTION _____

THANK-YOU WRITTEN BY _____
_____ DATE SENT ☐

NAME _____
GIFT DESCRIPTION _____

THANK-YOU WRITTEN BY _____
_____ DATE SENT ☐

NAME _____
GIFT DESCRIPTION _____

THANK-YOU WRITTEN BY _____
_____ DATE SENT ☐

NAME _____
GIFT DESCRIPTION _____

THANK-YOU WRITTEN BY _____
_____ DATE SENT ☐

Giving & Receiving Gifts

* * * * *

NAME	NAME
GIFT DESCRIPTION	GIFT DESCRIPTION

THANK-YOU WRITTEN BY _____ THANK-YOU WRITTEN BY _____
　　　　　　　　　　　　DATE SENT ☐　　　　　　　　　　　　　　　DATE SENT ☐

NAME　　　　　　　　　　　　　　　　　　　NAME
GIFT DESCRIPTION　　　　　　　　　　　　　　GIFT DESCRIPTION

THANK-YOU WRITTEN BY _____ THANK-YOU WRITTEN BY _____
　　　　　　　　　　　　DATE SENT ☐　　　　　　　　　　　　　　　DATE SENT ☐

NAME　　　　　　　　　　　　　　　　　　　NAME
GIFT DESCRIPTION　　　　　　　　　　　　　　GIFT DESCRIPTION

THANK-YOU WRITTEN BY _____ THANK-YOU WRITTEN BY _____
　　　　　　　　　　　　DATE SENT ☐　　　　　　　　　　　　　　　DATE SENT ☐

NAME　　　　　　　　　　　　　　　　　　　NAME
GIFT DESCRIPTION　　　　　　　　　　　　　　GIFT DESCRIPTION

THANK-YOU WRITTEN BY _____ THANK-YOU WRITTEN BY _____
　　　　　　　　　　　　DATE SENT ☐　　　　　　　　　　　　　　　DATE SENT ☐

NAME　　　　　　　　　　　　　　　　　　　NAME
GIFT DESCRIPTION　　　　　　　　　　　　　　GIFT DESCRIPTION

THANK-YOU WRITTEN BY _____ THANK-YOU WRITTEN BY _____
　　　　　　　　　　　　DATE SENT ☐　　　　　　　　　　　　　　　DATE SENT ☐

NAME　　　　　　　　　　　　　　　　　　　NAME
GIFT DESCRIPTION　　　　　　　　　　　　　　GIFT DESCRIPTION

THANK-YOU WRITTEN BY _____ THANK-YOU WRITTEN BY _____
　　　　　　　　　　　　DATE SENT ☐　　　　　　　　　　　　　　　DATE SENT ☐

Giving & Receiving Gifts

* * * * *

Name	Name
Gift Description	Gift Description
Thank-you written by _____ Date Sent ☐	Thank-you written by _____ Date Sent ☐

Name	Name
Gift Description	Gift Description
Thank-you written by _____ Date Sent ☐	Thank-you written by _____ Date Sent ☐

Name	Name
Gift Description	Gift Description
Thank-you written by _____ Date Sent ☐	Thank-you written by _____ Date Sent ☐

Name	Name
Gift Description	Gift Description
Thank-you written by _____ Date Sent ☐	Thank-you written by _____ Date Sent ☐

Name	Name
Gift Description	Gift Description
Thank-you written by _____ Date Sent ☐	Thank-you written by _____ Date Sent ☐

Name	Name
Gift Description	Gift Description
Thank-you written by _____ Date Sent ☐	Thank-you written by _____ Date Sent ☐

Name	Name
Gift Description	Gift Description
Thank-you written by _____ Date Sent ☐	Thank-you written by _____ Date Sent ☐

Giving & Receiving Gifts

* * * * *

NAME _____ NAME _____
GIFT DESCRIPTION _____ GIFT DESCRIPTION _____
_____ _____
THANK-YOU WRITTEN BY _____ THANK-YOU WRITTEN BY _____
_____ DATE SENT ☐ _____ DATE SENT ☐

NAME _____ NAME _____
GIFT DESCRIPTION _____ GIFT DESCRIPTION _____
_____ _____
THANK-YOU WRITTEN BY _____ THANK-YOU WRITTEN BY _____
_____ DATE SENT ☐ _____ DATE SENT ☐

NAME _____ NAME _____
GIFT DESCRIPTION _____ GIFT DESCRIPTION _____
_____ _____
THANK-YOU WRITTEN BY _____ THANK-YOU WRITTEN BY _____
_____ DATE SENT ☐ _____ DATE SENT ☐

NAME _____ NAME _____
GIFT DESCRIPTION _____ GIFT DESCRIPTION _____
_____ _____
THANK-YOU WRITTEN BY _____ THANK-YOU WRITTEN BY _____
_____ DATE SENT ☐ _____ DATE SENT ☐

NAME _____ NAME _____
GIFT DESCRIPTION _____ GIFT DESCRIPTION _____
_____ _____
THANK-YOU WRITTEN BY _____ THANK-YOU WRITTEN BY _____
_____ DATE SENT ☐ _____ DATE SENT ☐

NAME _____ NAME _____
GIFT DESCRIPTION _____ GIFT DESCRIPTION _____
_____ _____
THANK-YOU WRITTEN BY _____ THANK-YOU WRITTEN BY _____
_____ DATE SENT ☐ _____ DATE SENT ☐

Giving & Receiving Gifts

* * * * *

NAME _____
GIFT DESCRIPTION _____

THANK-YOU WRITTEN BY _____
                                    DATE SENT ☐

NAME _____
GIFT DESCRIPTION _____

THANK-YOU WRITTEN BY _____
                                    DATE SENT ☐

NAME _____
GIFT DESCRIPTION _____

THANK-YOU WRITTEN BY _____
                                    DATE SENT ☐

NAME _____
GIFT DESCRIPTION _____

THANK-YOU WRITTEN BY _____
                                    DATE SENT ☐

NAME _____
GIFT DESCRIPTION _____

THANK-YOU WRITTEN BY _____
                                    DATE SENT ☐

NAME _____
GIFT DESCRIPTION _____

THANK-YOU WRITTEN BY _____
                                    DATE SENT ☐

NAME _____
GIFT DESCRIPTION _____

THANK-YOU WRITTEN BY _____
                                    DATE SENT ☐

NAME _____
GIFT DESCRIPTION _____

THANK-YOU WRITTEN BY _____
                                    DATE SENT ☐

NAME _____
GIFT DESCRIPTION _____

THANK-YOU WRITTEN BY _____
                                    DATE SENT ☐

NAME _____
GIFT DESCRIPTION _____

THANK-YOU WRITTEN BY _____
                                    DATE SENT ☐

NAME _____
GIFT DESCRIPTION _____

THANK-YOU WRITTEN BY _____
                                    DATE SENT ☐

NAME _____
GIFT DESCRIPTION _____

THANK-YOU WRITTEN BY _____
                                    DATE SENT ☐

NAME _____
GIFT DESCRIPTION _____

THANK-YOU WRITTEN BY _____
                                    DATE SENT ☐

NAME _____
GIFT DESCRIPTION _____

THANK-YOU WRITTEN BY _____
                                    DATE SENT ☐

Giving & Receiving Gifts

* * * * *

NAME _____
GIFT DESCRIPTION _____
_____
THANK-YOU WRITTEN BY _____
_____ DATE SENT ☐

NAME _____
GIFT DESCRIPTION _____
_____
THANK-YOU WRITTEN BY _____
_____ DATE SENT ☐

NAME _____
GIFT DESCRIPTION _____
_____
THANK-YOU WRITTEN BY _____
_____ DATE SENT ☐

NAME _____
GIFT DESCRIPTION _____
_____
THANK-YOU WRITTEN BY _____
_____ DATE SENT ☐

NAME _____
GIFT DESCRIPTION _____
_____
THANK-YOU WRITTEN BY _____
_____ DATE SENT ☐

NAME _____
GIFT DESCRIPTION _____
_____
THANK-YOU WRITTEN BY _____
_____ DATE SENT ☐

NAME _____
GIFT DESCRIPTION _____
_____
THANK-YOU WRITTEN BY _____
_____ DATE SENT ☐

NAME _____
GIFT DESCRIPTION _____
_____
THANK-YOU WRITTEN BY _____
_____ DATE SENT ☐

NAME _____
GIFT DESCRIPTION _____
_____
THANK-YOU WRITTEN BY _____
_____ DATE SENT ☐

NAME _____
GIFT DESCRIPTION _____
_____
THANK-YOU WRITTEN BY _____
_____ DATE SENT ☐

NAME _____
GIFT DESCRIPTION _____
_____
THANK-YOU WRITTEN BY _____
_____ DATE SENT ☐

NAME _____
GIFT DESCRIPTION _____
_____
THANK-YOU WRITTEN BY _____
_____ DATE SENT ☐

NAME _____
GIFT DESCRIPTION _____
_____
THANK-YOU WRITTEN BY _____
_____ DATE SENT ☐

NAME _____
GIFT DESCRIPTION _____
_____
THANK-YOU WRITTEN BY _____
_____ DATE SENT ☐

Giving & Receiving Gifts

Parties

✳ ✳ ✳ ✳ ✳

Celebrating Your Nuptials

From the moment you become engaged, there's a reason to throw a party, then another, and another, leading up to and continuing after you've spoken your vows and driven off in a car, tin cans scraping the pavement. Some of these festivities will be thrown for you, some will be hosted by friends. Still others may be given by the two of you as a couple, by the bride, or by the groom.

    The first opportunity for an event is, of course, the Engagement Party. Then, as the wedding date approaches, someone may offer to throw a shower. (In days of old this was called the "bridal shower," but in this brave new world, showers often include the groom and other menfolk.) It's inappropriate for a shower to be hosted by a member of the bride or groom's immediate family, so we won't discuss such festivities here. The parties that will be addressed are the Bridesmaids' Party, the Rehearsal Dinner, and the Gift-Opening Brunch.

The Engagement Party

This is the first official gathering of both sets of parents and siblings. The two of you may host it, or it may be held at the home of a parent or other close relative. You'll want to limit the number of guests and create an intimate atmosphere. This is a time for people to get to know one another (for better or worse).

Hosted By

_____

Location   **Date & Time**

_____

_____

Food & Beverages

_____

_____

_____

_____

Notes

_____

_____

_____

_____

Guests

_____

_____

_____

_____

_____

_____

_____

* * * * *

The Bridesmaids' Party

This may be a tea, a luncheon, or dinner served at a special restaurant or at the bride's home. It could be strictly a girl thing—a fancy get-together after the final dress fittings, with the bride treating her attendants to lunch and giving them each a gift. "Spa days" are another possibility: Everyone gets a facial or a manicure followed by a healthy lunch or decadent dessert. Or you could have a bridesmaids' dinner party that includes your attendants' spouses or dates. (Of course, then you'd have to invite the groom, and maybe he'd want to invite the groomsmen, and their dates. See how quickly these things get out of hand?) If you do limit it to just the girls, consider including close female relatives and soon-to-be relatives.

Hosted By

Location   **Date & Time**

Food & Beverages

Notes

Guests

* * * * *

The Rehearsal Dinner

The Rehearsal Dinner is also known as the "Groom's Dinner," because it's often hosted by the groom's parents. After the rehearsal, the wedding party gathers—along with close relatives from both sides of the family—to drink wine, exchange amusing anecdotes, and demonstrate their ability to chew food while answering questions about their individual lines of work. You may want to invite special friends and relatives who have traveled great distances to come to your wedding, since this may be the only opportunity you have to speak three or more full sentences to them.

HOSTED BY

LOCATION   DATE & TIME

FOOD & BEVERAGES

NOTES

GUESTS

Parties

✶ ✶ ✶ ✶

The Gift-Opening Brunch

This is a recent innovation, a sign of the times. In days of old, the wedded couple took off in their automobile, boarded a plane, and spent two blissful weeks in Hawaii doing things they had never before done. At least, that was the fantasy version of the scenario. Back then, a newlywed couple wanted privacy, for obvious reasons. But now, with so many couples cohabiting before marriage (along with the tendency to postpone the honeymoon until days, weeks, or even months after the ceremony), post-wedding privacy is not always a concern.

The Gift-Opening Brunch provides the solution to a modern-day problem: the acrimoniously divorced couple. As one recent bride relates, after friends of her family went through a bitter divorce, the ex-wife didn't want to be in the same room with her ex-husband. The bride had grown up with this couple, who were friends of her parents. She wanted both of them to be included in her wedding festivities, and so made a discreet call to the ex-husband. It turned out that he wasn't that enthusiastic about attending weddings (go figure) and would prefer to attend the post-wedding party. His ex-wife attended the nuptials, and they all lived happily ever after, each carefully out of view of the other.

The brunch can be hosted at the home of parents or the newlywed couple, although this might require a Herculean effort. If you've rented a resort for a weekend of wedding-related events, the brunch could be held in a private suite, in the lodge or at the restaurant, and serve as the last hurrah before everyone heads home. Attire is casual and food is served buffet-style. The couple opens wedding gifts, with appropriate oohs and aahs from friends and family.

HOSTED BY

_____

LOCATION   DATE & TIME

_____

FOOD & BEVERAGES

_____

_____

_____

_____

_____

_____

_____

_____

_____

_____

Parties

* * * * *

BRUNCH GUESTS   **NOTES**

Parties

Your Honeymoon

✶ ✶ ✶ ✶ ✶

Bon Voyage

Finally—a chance to be alone together. Even if financial constraints or work responsibilities will prevent you from taking a week's vacation in the tropics, at the very least you'll want to reserve a hotel suite for your wedding night.

   Most grooms take it upon themselves to make travel arrangements for the honeymoon. But it's probably not a good idea for the groom to surprise his bride with where they're going, since his idea of a great trip might be her vacation nightmare. Instead, make your honeymoon plans together.

   Take some time to think about all the possible destinations: an all-inclusive resort in Jamaica or Hawaii, a road trip through Ireland, or a cottage in the woods with a fireplace and Jacuzzi. Even trips that seem prohibitively expensive may be possible if you travel during the off-season. In addition to your fantasy destinations, talk to each other about your personal vacation styles. Do you prefer action-packed adventure or lying on the beach with a stack of bestsellers?

As a reminder, turn back to the first section of this planner. See how much you budgeted for your honeymoon?

RECORD THAT AMOUNT HERE: $ _____

Just something to keep in mind.

Honeymoon Ideas

* * * * *

If you need help generating ideas, check area bookstores for books and magazines related to travel, or call your local department of tourism to request directories of hotels and resorts in the state.

An experienced travel agent can help you choose the perfect destination and take care of almost every detail—at no cost to you. (Agents earn commissions from airlines and hotels.) Even if your plans are set, a good agent can offer suggestions and may know about festivities or events you wouldn't want to miss.

Don't make reservations solely based on a brochure, especially if you're traveling out of the country. It's best to follow the recommendation of a friend who's recently visited the place, and even then, call and find out if there will be any construction work or whether it's monsoon season during the time you'll be honeymooning. When room reservations are made, ask about the view—an oceanside room will be more expensive than one that faces a chicken coop. Deposits may be nonrefundable. Beware of deals that sound too good to be true.

Wedding Night Bliss

Even if you won't be leaving for your honeymoon right away, reserve a room at a hotel or inn for the evening of your nuptials. Be sure to mention that it'll be your wedding night—so they can give you free stuff if they want to.

HOTEL

ADDRESS

DIRECTIONS FROM RECEPTION SITE

PHONE   CONFIRMATION #

RATE

Honeymoon Possibilities

OPTION # 1

Place

AGENT OR RESERVATION

PHONE   DESTINATION

ACCOMMODATIONS

LENGTH OF STAY

Estimated Cost

WHAT'S INCLUDED IN THAT COST

Your Honeymoon

* * * * *

TRANSPORTATION COSTS (ROUNDTRIP AIRFARE FOR TWO, CAR RENTAL, GAS)

_____

_____

Additional Expenses
MEALS OUTSIDE THE HOTEL

BREAKFASTS

LUNCHES

DINNERS

ESTIMATED COST OF MEALS _____
ENTERTAINMENT

SHOPPING & SOUVENIRS

MISC. (TIPS, TAXES, ETC.)

Total Est. Cost $ _____

OPTION # 2

Place

AGENT OR RESERVATION

PHONE _____ DESTINATION

ACCOMMODATIONS

LENGTH OF STAY

Estimated Cost

WHAT'S INCLUDED IN THAT COST

_____

_____

TRANSPORTATION COSTS (ROUNDTRIP AIRFARE FOR TWO, CAR RENTAL, GAS)

_____

_____

Additional Expenses
MEALS OUTSIDE THE HOTEL

BREAKFASTS

LUNCHES

DINNERS

ESTIMATED COST OF MEALS _____
ENTERTAINMENT

SHOPPING & SOUVENIRS

MISC. (TIPS, TAXES, ETC.)

Total Est. Cost $ _____

Your Honeymoon

* * * * *

Option # 3

Place

Agent or Reservation

Phone   Destination

Accommodations

Length of Stay

Estimated Cost

What's Included in that Cost

Transportation Costs (roundtrip airfare for two, car rental, gas)

Additional Expenses
Meals outside the hotel

Breakfasts

Lunches

Dinners

Estimated Cost of Meals

Entertainment

Shopping & Souvenirs

Misc. (Tips, Taxes, etc.)

Total Est. Cost $

Information & Itinerary

Once you've decided on a trip, record specific travel information below. (Give a copy of your itinerary and numbers where you can be reached to an individual who promises to leave you alone unless there's an emergency.)

Travel Agent

Phone

Airline & Flight Number

Departure Date & Time

Return Flight Number

Departure Date & Time

Total Airfare $
Rental Car Agency   Phone   Res #

Car Rental Rate   cost/day+cents/mile.+Ins.

Total Cost $
Accommodations

Phone   Res#

Rate

Your Honeymoon

ITINERARY

in items as you think of them. Receive a piece of lingerie as a shower gift? Throw it in the bag (after you've written the thank-you note, of course). By employing this method, you should be able to finish packing in a few minutes' time just before you go. Below are some things you don't want to forget. They're listed in no particular order of importance. With these few items, a person can take on the world.

- *Tickets*
- *Passport or visa (not necessary for travel to Canada, Mexico, and some foreign countries, although you'll probably need to bring a copy of your birth certificate and a driver's license— check with your travel agent)*
- *Traveler's checks, credit card, ATM card, cash (lots of small bills), and checkbook*
- *List of numbers: traveler's checks, credit cards and checking account, along with phone numbers to call in case these items are lost or stolen. Keep this list in a bag separate from the credit cards, traveler's checks and checkbook*
- *Driver's license*
- *Bathing suit*
- *Robe or loungewear*
- *Toothbrush & toothpaste*
- *Corkscrew*
- *Aspirin, antacids & prescription medication*

What to Pack

A week before your trip, set your open suitcase on the bedroom floor. Keep a list of everything you intend to bring (you know— camera, bikini, playing cards, Band-aids) next to your luggage. That way, you can toss

Your Honeymoon

Notes

Resources

RESOURCES

Resources

✶ ✶ ✶ ✶ ✶

Apparel & Accessories

Ardour
1115 First Avenue
Seattle, WA 98101
206/292-0660

Beverly Hunnicutt
608 West Crockett
Seattle, WA 98119
206/283-0655

The Bridal Garden
10 Lakeshore Plaza
Kirkland, WA 98033
425/889-2151

Boutique Christiane
Forum Plaza
10129 Main Street
Bellevue, WA 98004
425/451-1171

Cicada
723 East Pike Street
Seattle, WA 98122
206/325-2595

Debra Masson for Bella
12929 170th Avenue NE
Redmond, WA 98052
425/885-0271

Elaine's of Edmonds
610 Main Street
Edmonds, WA 98020
425/778-1814

I Do Bridal
Wallingford Center
1815 N. 45th Street,
Seattle, WA 98103
206/633-7926

Isadora's
1915 First Avenue
Seattle, WA 98101
206/441-7711

Knar Custom Design
127A Lake Street South
Kirkland, WA 98033
425/827-5042

la belle mariée
8433 122nd Avenue NE
Kirkland, WA 98033
425/889-8606

Madame & Co.
1901 10th Avenue West
Seattle, WA 98119
206/281-7908

Marcella's la Boutique
1304 Western Avenue
Seattle, WA 98101
206/467-8693

Nordstrom
1501 Fifth Avenue
Seattle, WA 98101
206/628-2111

Olivine Atelier
5344 Ballard Avenue NW
Seattle, WA 98107
206/706-4188

Susan Trenery
1437 9th Avenue West
Seattle, WA 98119
206/282-6570

Victoria's Bridal, Inc.
7106 Woodlawn Ave. NE
Seattle, WA 98115
206/517-2909

Cakes

B & O Espresso
204 Belmont East
Seattle, WA 98102
206/322-5028

Hollyhock Bakery
518 15th Avenue East
Seattle, WA 98112
206/322-1152

Great Cakes & Edible Monuments
2545 152nd Ave. N.E.
Redmond, WA 98052
425/882-0896

Amazing Cakes
14934 N.E. 31st Circle
Redmond, WA 98052
425/869-2992

Patisserie Alena
8218 S.E. 26th Street
Mercer Island, WA 98040
206/230-6488

Caterers

CaterArts
2501 North Northlake Way
Seattle, WA 98103
206/632-2200

The Harvest Vine
2701 East Madison
Seattle, WA 98112
206/320-9771

Lisa Dupar Catering
17825 N.E. 65th Street
Redmond, WA 98052
425/881-3250

Ravishing Radish
81 Vine Street, Suite 100
Seattle, WA 98121
206/448-6886

The Upper Crust
3231 20th Avenue West
Seattle, WA 98199
206/283-2551

* * * * *

Floral Designers

Aaron Diamond's Floral Masters
2301 First Avenue
Seattle, WA 98121
206/448-7959

Athena Flora
4610 148th Street SW
Lynnwood, WA 98037
425/742-0758

Bloomers of Bellevue
10149 1/2 Main Street
Bellevue, WA 98004
425/454-7735

Emilie Clark
Bellevue Place
800 Bellevue Way NE
Bellevue, WA 98004
425/455-2122

Esprit de Fleur
P.O. Box 31817
Seattle, WA 98103
206/547-7271

Fena Flowers
12815 NE 124th Street
Suite K
Kirkland, WA 98034
425/825-8181

Fiori Floral & Garden
512 East Pike Street
Seattle, WA 98122
206/329-3944

Fleurish
1411 34th Avenue
Seattle, WA 98122
206/322-1602

Martha E. Harris
4218 E. Madison Street
Seattle, WA 98112
206/568-0347

Nature's Inc.
435 15th Avenue East
Seattle, WA 98112
206/322-1558

Rosengarten
2134 Third Avenue
Seattle, WA 98121
206/448-7673

Formal Wear

Black Tie Formal Wear
Bellevue and
additional locations
425/775-0421

Mr. Formal
Bellevue and
additional locations
425/453-2227

Shafrans
4546 California Ave. SW
Seattle, WA 98116
206/937-6720

Winters
Formal Wear
310 Broadway East
Seattle, WA 98102
206/324-3171
Bellevue Square
425/455-3181

Honeymoon Destinations

The Coeur d'Alene
Resort
P.O. Box 7200
Coeur d'Alene, ID 83816
800/688-5253

Columbia Gorge
Hotel
4000 Westcliff Drive
Hood River, OR 97031
800/345-1921

The Empress Hotel
721 Government Street
Victoria, B.C. V8W1W5
250/384-8111

Four Sisters Inns
P.O. Box 3073
Monterey, CA 93942
800/234-1425

✶ ✶ ✶ ✶ ✶

Roche Harbor
Resort
P.O. Box 4001
Roche Harbor, WA 98250
800/451-8910

Rosario Resort
One Rosario Way
Eastsound, WA 98245
360/376-2222

Salish Lodge & Spa
P.O. Box 1109
Snoqualmie, WA 98065
425/888-2556

Stephanie Inn
P.O. Box 219
Cannon Beach, OR 97110
800/377-4100

Whistler Resort
4010 Whistler Way
Whistler, B.C.
VON 1B4
604/932-3928

Hotels

The Alexis Hotel
First & Madison
Seattle, WA 98101
206/624-4844

Hotel Monaco
1101 Fourth Avenue
Seattle, WA 98101
206/621-1770

Hotel Vintage Park
1100 Fifth Ave.
Seattle, WA 98101
206/624-8000

Inn at Harbor Steps
1221 First Avenue
Seattle, WA 98101
206/748-0973

The Sorrento Hotel
900 Madison Street
Seattle, WA 98104
206/622-6400

Ice Carving

Creative Ice
Carvings
P.O. Box 54203
Redondo, WA 98054
253/941-7248

Invitations, Stationery

Bellevue Art &
Frame
1924 116th Avenue NE
Bellevue, WA 98004
425/453-8959

de Medici Ming
Fine Paper
1222-A First Avenue
Seattle, WA 98101
206/624-1983

Of the Earth
Bemis Building
55 Atlantic Street #408
Seattle, WA 98134
206/464-0664

Papertree
149 Bellevue Square
Bellevue, WA 98004
425/451-8035

Papyrus
241A Bellevue Square
Bellevue, WA 98004
425/451-4802
2660 NE University Village
Seattle, WA 98105
206/523-0055
For other locations
800/872-7978

Real Card Company
2814 E. Madison Street
Seattle, WA 98112
206/325-1854

Silberman Brown Stationers
10220 NE 8th Street
Bellevue, WA 98004
425/455-3665
1322 Fifth Avenue
Seattle, WA 98101
206/292-9404

Stylus Paper & Pen
4710 University Village Place NE
Seattle, WA 98105
206/523-2106

★ ★ ★ ★ ★

JEWELERS

Carroll's Fine Jewelry
1427 Fourth Avenue
Seattle, WA 98101
206/622-9191

European Creations
1424 Fourth Avenue
Suite 4E
Seattle, WA 98101
206/628-0338

Joseph's Jewelry
10129 Main Street
Bellevue, WA 98004
425/453-8258

Jose Hernandez Jeweler
10246 Main Street
Bellevue, WA 98004
425/451-0244

Menashe & Sons Jewelers
4532 California Ave. SW
Seattle, WA 98116
206/932-4272

Scandia Jewelers
1011 First Avenue
Seattle, WA 98104
206/682-7464

Turgeon Raine
1407 Fifth Avenue
Seattle, WA 98101
206/447-9488

LIMOUSINES

British Motor Coach
761 Aloha Street, Suite B
Seattle, WA 98109
206/283-6600

European Limousine
19561 144th Avenue NE
Woodinville, WA 98072
206/223-1701

LINGERIE

Boisvert Lingerie
10028 Main Street
Bellevue, WA 98004
425/451-9266

Nancy Meyer Fine Lingerie
1398 Fifth Avenue
Seattle, WA 98101
206/625-9200

PHOTOGRAPHERS & VIDEOGRAPHERS

Carol Harrold Photography
4533 49th Avenue SW
Seattle, WA 98116
206/938-4674

Curt Smith Photography
P.O. Box 1886
Kingston, WA 98346
360/297-8938

* * * * *

*Curtis Rhodes
Photography*
914 NW 80th Street
Seattle, WA 98117
206/782-3681

Daniel Sheehan
3516 Carr Place North
Seattle, WA 98103
206/633-0656

*Dani Weiss
Photography*
316 31st Avenue #3
Seattle, WA 98122
206/760-3336

*Hudson Design
Portraits*
16627 Benson Road S
Renton, WA 98055
425/271-9709

*Jessica Young
Photography*
2900 NE Blakely Street
Studio 4
Seattle, WA 98105
206/522-3758

Jill Labberton
11 West McGraw Street
Seattle, WA 98119
206/283-1038

*Joan Barker
Photography*
1916 Pike Place #236
Seattle, WA 98101
206/298-0229

Laszlo Photography
23103 NE 134th Circle
Brush Prairie, WA 98606
360/882-7695

MBC Video
14415 NE 64th Street
Redmond, WA 98052
425/885-7934

*Melanie Blair
Photography*
325 2nd Avenue West
Seattle, WA 98119
206/285-7717

Paul Sanders
Photography
11738 Kallgren Road
Bainbridge Is., WA 98110
206/780-5152

*Robin Layton
Photography*
2229 First Avenue West
Seattle, WA 98119
206/285-8343

Stephanie Cristalli
9211 Phinney Avenue N
Seattle, WA 98103
206/783-8985

Real Estate

Moira Holley
w/ John L. Scott
206/660-4787

Mary Alice Shea
w/ Windermere
206/448-4840

Reception sites

Argosy Cruises
Pier 55
Seattle, WA 98101
206/623-1445

The Bacon Mansion
959 Broadway East
Seattle, WA 98102
206/329-1864

*Bell Harbor
International
Conference Center*
2211 Alaskan Way, Pier 66
Seattle, WA 98121
206/441-6666

Bellevue Club Hotel
11200 SE 6th Street
Bellevue, WA 98004
425/454-4424

*Columbia
Tower Club*
701 5th Ave. Suite 7600
Seattle, WA 98104
206/622-2010

Crowne Plaza Hotel
1113 6th Avenue
Seattle, WA 98101
206/464-1980

Resources
117

* * * * *

*Daughters of
the American
Revolution*
800 East Roy Street
Seattle, WA 98102
206/323-0600

*Doubletree
Hotel Bellevue*
300 112th Avenue SE
Bellevue, WA 98004
425/455-1300

*Doubletree
Hotel SeaTac*
18740 Pacific Highway S
Seattle, WA 98188
206/433-1888

Echo Falls
20414 121st Ave. SE
Snohomish, WA 98296
425/454-2800

*Embassy Suites
Bellevue*
3225 158th Ave. SE
Bellevue, WA 98008
425/644-2500

Fairview Club
2022 Boren Avenue
Seattle, WA 98121
206/623-9003

*Four Seasons
Olympic*
411 University Street
Seattle, WA 98101
206/621-1700

The Golf Club
at Newcastle
7555 155th Ave. SE
Newcastle, WA 98058

Grand Atrium
1201 3rd Ave., Suite 150
Seattle, WA 98101
206/224-7030

Hotel Edgewater
2411 Alaskan Way, Pier 67
Seattle, WA 98121
206/269-4550
See ad on page 69

*Hyatt Regency
Bellevue*
900 Bellevue Way NE
Bellevue, WA 98004
425/462-1234

Indian Summer Golf
and Country Club
5900 Troon Lane SE
Olympia, WA 98501

*The Inn at
Semi-ah-moo*
9565 Semi-ah-moo Pkwy.
Blaine, WA 98230
360/371-2000

Kiana Lodge
14976 Sandy Hook Rd. NE
Poulsbo, WA 98370
206/282-4633

*The Kline-Galland
Mansion*
1605 17th Avenue
Seattle, WA 98112
206/328-0163

*Landmark
Convention Center*
47 St. Helens Avenue
Tacoma, WA 98402
253/272-2042

M.V. Skansonia
2505 N Northlake Way
Seattle, WA 98103
206/545-9109

*Mayflower
Park Hotel*
405 Olive Way
Seattle, WA 98101
206/382-6991

*The Meeting Place
at Pike Place Market*
93 Pike Street Suite 307
Seattle, WA 98101
206/447-9994

*Mill Creek
Country Club*
15500 Country Club Dr.
Mill Creek, WA 98012
425/743-1444

*Monte Villa
Farmhouse*
3300 Monte Villa Pkwy.
Bothell, WA 98021
425/485-6115

Resources

* * * * *

Museum of Flight
9404 E Marginal Way S
Seattle, WA 98108
206/764-5706

Old Morris Farm
105 West Morris
Coupeville, WA 98239
800/936-6586

*Palisades
Restaurant*
Elliott Bay Marina
2601 West Marina Pl.
Seattle, WA 98199
206/285-5865

*Renaissance
Madison Hotel*
515 Madison Street
Seattle, WA 98104
206/583-0300

Robinswood House
2432 148th Ave SE
Bellevue, WA 98007
425/455-7850

*The Seattle
Space Needle*
Seattle Center
219 Fourth Avenue
Seattle, WA 98109
206/443-9800

*Sheraton Seattle
Hotel & Towers*
1400 Sixth Avenue
Seattle, WA 98101
206/621-9000

*Shilshole Bay
Beach Club*
6413 Seaview Ave. NW
Seattle, WA 98107
206/706-0257

Shumway Mansion
11410 99th Place NE
Kirkland, WA 98033
425/823-2303

Silverlake Winery
17721 132nd Ave. NE
Woodinville, WA 98072
425/486-1900

*Stimson-Green
Mansion*
1204 Minor Aveune
Seattle, WA 98101
206/624-0474

The Tacoma Club
1201 Pacific Ave.
Suite 1601
Tacoma, WA 98402
253/272-3218

Westin Seattle
1900 Fifth Avenue
Seattle, WA 98101
206/728-1000

*West Coast
Bellevue Hotel*
625 116th Avenue NE
Bellevue, WA 98004
425/455-9444

Restaurants

Canlis
2576 Aurora Avenue N
Seattle, WA 98109
206/283-3313

*El Gaucho
Restaurant*
2505 First Avenue
Seattle, WA 98121
206/728-1337

Kaspars
19 West Harrison
Seattle, WA 98119
206/298-0123

The Painted Table
92 Madison Street
Seattle, WA 98101
206/624-3646

Palace Kitchen
2030 Fifth Avenue
Seattle, WA 98121
206/448-2001

Rover's
2808 East Madison
Seattle, WA 98112
206/325-7442

Saleh al Lago
6804 Greenlake Way N
Seattle, WA 98115
206/524-4044

*****

Sazerac
1101 Fourth Ave.
Seattle, WA 98101
206/624-7755
See ad on page 61

*Szmania's
Restaurant*
3321 W. McGraw Street
Seattle, WA 98199
206/284-7305

Tulio Ristorante
1100 Fifth Avenue
Seattle, WA 98101
206/624-5500

Yarrow Bay Grill
1270 Carillon Point
Kirkland, WA 98033
425/803-2941

Spas & Salons

Habitude
5350 Ballard Avenue NW
Seattle, WA 98107
206/782-2898

Jaroslava Day Spa
1413 Fourth Avenue
Seattle, WA 98101
206/623-3336

Salon Joseph
600 West McGraw Street
Seattle, WA 98119
206/285-1113

Spa Csaba
1250 Carillon Point
Kirkland, WA 98033
425/803-9000

Ummelina
1425 Fourth Avenue
Seattle, WA 98101
206/624-1370

Tabletop, Gifts & Accessories

The Bon Marche
Third & Pine Street
Seattle, WA 98181
206/506-6000
Bridal Registry:
206/506-6995

Choice Linens
113 Battery
Seattle, WA 98121
206/325-0111

Cook's World
2900 NE Blakely Street
Seattle, WA 98105
206/528-8192

*Custom Chair
Covers*
28 University Place NE
Auburn, WA 98002
253/939-7119

Egbert's
2231 First Avenue
Seattle, WA 98121
206/728-5682

Fireworks Gallery
University Village
206/527-2858
also at Westlake Center,
Pioneer Square,
Bellevue Square

Great Jones Home
1921 Second Avenue
Seattle, WA 98101
206/448-9405

The Homing Instinct
1622 Queen Anne
Avenue North
Seattle, WA 98109
206/281-9260
See ad on page 72

JC Penney
Various locations
206/246-0850

Kasala
1505 Western Avenue
Seattle, WA 98101
206/623-7795

Laguna Pottery
116 South Washington
Seattle, WA 98104
206/682-6162

Masins
220 2nd Avenue South
Seattle, WA 98104
206/622-5606
10245 Main Street
Bellevue, WA 98004
425/450-9999

Mondeo
1200 Western Avenue
Seattle, WA 98101
206/622-9426

Mrs. Cooks
2810 NE University Village
Seattle, WA 98105
206/525-5008

Partners in Time
1332 Sixth Avenue
Seattle, WA 98101
206/623-4218

Porcelain Gallery
2426 32nd Avenue West
Seattle, WA 98199
206/284-5893

Sundance
2683 NE University Village
Seattle, WA 98105
206/729-0750

Table Top Shop
2664 NE University Village
Seattle, WA 98105
206/526-8480
Bellevue
425/454-7322

Zanadia
Wallingford Center
1815 North 45th Street
Seattle, WA 98103
206/547-0884

* * * * *

Bridal Shows

Seattle Wedding Show
18027 Hwy. 99 Suite B1
Lynnwood, WA 98037
425/744-6509

Wedding Consultants

Signature Affairs
600 Queen Anne Avenue
Suite 104
Seattle, WA 98109
206/282-8664

Resources

Notes

✳ ✳ ✳ ✳

Notes

* * * * *

Notes

Notes

✶ ✶ ✶ ✶

Notes

✳ ✳ ✳ ✳

NOTES

Notes